What's Age Got To Do With It?

Volume II

&

Kelly Ferrin

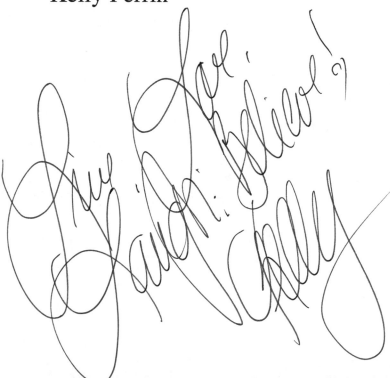

Consult your physician before beginning any fitness program. The contents presented herein are not intended as therapy, recommendations, or as substitutes for treatment by a physician or other health-care professional. The accounts described in this book are only the personal experiences of those listed.

Red Zone Publishing
1509 N. Milwaukee Avenue, Libertyville, IL 60048

Cover design: Jamie Mattock, Flow Motion
Interior design: Melanie Springer, Red Zone Marketing

Photograph on Page 201, courtesy Detroit Free Press
Page 204, courtesy Los Angeles Lakers

ALTI Publishing
Excerpts from What's Age Got To Do With It? Volume I
courtesy of Alti Publishing (858) 452-7703

Printed in The United States
10 9 8 7 6 5 4 3 2 1

Ten Secrets to Ageless Living

& Never let age get in the way of life.

& Stay curious, explore, discover, and continue to learn
    new things.

& Play, have fun, be happy, and maintain a zest for life by
    being vital.

& Keep the brain and the body busy; stimulate the mind, eat
    healthy, exercise.

& Smile, laugh, maintain a sense of humor, and always stay
    young at heart.

& Have a positive attitude, outlook, and be optimistic to
    overcome challenges.

& Believe in yourself by having faith, hope, spirit, value,
    meaning and purpose.

& Stay connected, engaged, creative, and useful by
    continuing to contribute.

& Find fulfillment, peace, serenity, and self-esteem by
    giving back -- volunteer.

& Enjoy and cherish healthy relationships with loved ones,
    friends, and family.

The Ageless Golden Rule

Live long, live well, laugh often, love much . . .
And always enjoy life's journey.

Dedication

*To all those who believe age is just a number
and whose lives have inspired me
to share the secrets of what's possible with age.*

Acknowledgements

There are many who deserve thanks for making this project possible, including supportive family, friends, associates, and all those who shared their stories. Special thanks to the team at Red Zone Marketing who enabled me to clear the hurdles and get this project done; to Sandra O'Rourke and Alti Publishing for their continued support; and to my many business associates who have provided me the opportunity to share this message professionally.

Additionally I want to express my sincere gratitude to my family, who have not only served as inspirational role models, but who have also supported and cheered me on along this journey. To my husband Tim, who's never ending love and support, enables me to do my life's work. And to our loved ones upstairs who continue to guide and light my path in a spiritual way, I thank you for the gift and opportunity to help make a positive difference in the lives of others.

What's Age Got To Do With It?
Volume II

ℰℴ

Table of Contents

Introduction

Life Lessons

SuperSenior Celebs

SuperSeniors

SuperSeniors - The Best of Volume I

Introduction

ଚ୍ଚ

How old
would "old" be
if we didn't know
how old "old" was?

If we really believed age was just a number, think how differently we would live our lives. Who says you can't hang glide at 90, run hurdles at 80, be an entrepreneur at 70, or an adventurer at 60? What is "normal" for today's 70-, 80-, 90-, and 100-year olds? It's not about rocking chairs anymore -- more like rock climbing! Exploring, adventuring, volunteering, having a sense of meaning, purpose and a zest for life are ageless qualities that can be obtained at any age.

A definite trend is occurring -- aging is changing. People are living longer, healthier lives than ever before and this extraordinary phenomenon is forever changing both the way we look at aging and even the way we age ourselves. A new style of aging is also emerging as people determine what's really possible in their later years. The life cycle has changed and so have the rules. The majority of older adults today are healthy and happy and believe these are among the best years of their lives. They're not concerned with avoiding aging -- they've discovered the secrets by being and doing, and never letting age get in the way of living.

People are doing some extraordinary things as a result of living longer. In fact, so many are living their lives this way the question now becomes: Are these people really extraordinary ... or has this become ordinary? Research validates what's occurring in today's new older adult population. The scientific breakthroughs in healthcare and medical technology have enabled us to live longer, and current studies prove that we definitely play a significant role in determining not only how long we live, but perhaps more importantly, how well we live.

When I wrote the original *What's Age Got To Do With It?*, my interest was the same as it is today: to help people learn about living healthy, vital lives as long as possible to enjoy a positive quality of life. And from all the studies I've reviewed and interviews I've conducted since then, maintaining one's health and independence is still a priority for most people, particularly with age. There's certainly enough medical information available to teach people how to age well, but for some reason, healthy aging has yet to become a mainstream way of thinking. This fascinates me. Perhaps if we had a more positive image of aging, people would be more receptive to the role they play in their aging process and quality of life and start implementing the lifestyle behaviors that would make a difference in their lives.

It's all about choices -- which are often determined by our image of aging. This is a powerful concept because mindset, attitude and beliefs drive behaviors. So with aging now being redefined, it's time to change our thinking of what our later years can be since what we believe directly affects the choices we make, which therefore affects our health, longevity, and our lives.

There are definitely a variety of ways to age. It's no longer an inevitable time of decline. Yet because we've never been a long-lived society with millions of healthy older adults serving as role models like we have today, we've been conditioned to believe age is a time of decline. We age because we expect to age, since that's all we've ever known or believed was possible. Historically, the majority of aging studies were done exclusively on the sick and frail in nursing homes. But are those the only seniors there are? Of course not, yet because this was the side of aging predominantly studied, this became our entire image of aging. The positive aging images have been far and few between ... until now.

I've always believed there was another side of aging because I'd seen healthy, active, vital, and productive seniors who were the same age as those studied in institutions, but were living very different lives. Clearly it wasn't just chronological age -- other contributing factors affect how people live well in their later years and prevent much of the decline so many believed was just automatic with age.

As a golfer who became a gerontologist, I got into this field in a somewhat backwards way, but in a way that clearly identifies my passion for aging. At a very impressionable stage in my life, I spent a lot of time on the golf course with older adults and retirees. As a result, I started looking at aging in a completely different way. I saw healthy, active, vital people living their lives. When I got into the academic side of aging, all I read about were the problem sides of aging. I specifically remember stating that I had seen a whole other side of aging and if we were indeed becoming an aged society, we'd better start figuring out what's right with age instead of just focusing on what's wrong with it. The turning point came when I realized people in nursing homes were the same age as people on the golf course. Clearly there was something more than just age going on here.

At that point I knew there was a lot of work to be done in this field. For starters, we needed a more balanced perspective on aging. Recognizing we'd never been here before --

with the numbers of people living as long as they're living and living as well as they're living, this was completely uncharted territory for which there was no road map. In many ways this was a good thing because as a result, there were no rules. Yet at the same time, overcoming decades of negative images and outdated notions would likely be a huge challenge. We're actually just now learning what it means to live long and live well -- and we're discovering some fascinating new things.

To begin with, current statistics show that 95.8 percent of Americans age 65 to 74 live independently, yet at the introduction of Social Security in 1935, only 4 percent even survived past 65. Today, life expectancy is pushing 80, yet we're still calling 65 old. In the past fifteen years there's been a 15 percent decline in disabilities among people over age 85 -- which is also the fastest growing segment of the U.S. population.

The long-term studies on healthy aging are also providing a more positive perspective. According to the results of an on-going 25-year 'Successful Aging' study at Mt. Sinai Medical Center in New York, 70 percent of the characteristics of aging today are based on lifestyle, 30 percent on genetics. In looking at the ten leading health problems for people 65+, 80 percent are lifestyle related. They are not normal, automatic aspects of aging. There are 40-year olds with all the problems and 80-year olds with none of them. So lifestyle can prevent, postpone the onset and slow down the pain and debilitation of many of the conditions people generally blame on age. The reality is: the choices we make on a daily basis have a direct effect on how we age and therefore our quality of life.

This is exciting news because it means it's never too late to incorporate healthy activities into our lifestyle and benefit from them. The reality of this however is that now we face an entirely new challenge: the economic ramifications of longevity -- people outliving their money. Unfortunately, the majority of people have no idea how long they're likely going to live - let alone what it may cost them to do so. And with a healthcare system on the verge of collapse, it's essential for people to understand the health and wealth connection, and the role we each play in it. The healthier you are, the wealthier you are financially and physically -- meaning the less you'll spend on healthcare, so the happier, healthier, and wealthier you'll likely be - not to mention helping save the healthcare system which can only survive if this type of thinking is achieved. It's not the doctor's job to take care of us - it's our job to take care of us, and everyone needs to take more responsibility for both their health and their life.

But in order to achieve this, a new mindset may be needed first, because what we think is possible in our later years directly affects the choices we make, and thus our aging process. If we believe our later years can be a time of good health and vitality, then we're more likely to incorporate the lifestyle behaviors necessary to ensure this reality.

There is no magic formula to guarantee a long life filled with good health and happiness, but there are a variety of secrets that together can definitely increase our odds of getting older without getting old. Many in their later years are doing things people half their age can't do, and there are reasons why they can ... and why others can, too.

The entire concept of aging and retirement is changing. It's no longer a time of just sitting on the front porch or playing bingo. We're spending as much as 30 years in retirement, which can result in people doing a variety of different things. Yet the majority of people still spend more time planning a two-week vacation than they do the third of their life they'll spend retired. This is probably because most people anticipate having a good time on their vacation, but they're not so sure about this retirement stage. The reality is we've added 30 years to our life expectancy since the 1900s. Does that mean we're going to be older longer? No, it seems we're actually extending middle age. With people often feeling 10 to 15 years younger than their natural age, the new 70 today is more like 50 of yesterday.

Agelessness is seemingly something everybody's after. The reality however, is it comes from within -- it's a state of mind. Best of all, it's within each one of us -- an inner strength and spirit that is completely within our control. It's all about hope and keeping our pilot light lit. We aren't all going to do extraordinary things, but inspiring stories of others can instill hope and belief in all of us, which is perhaps the most beautiful gift of all -- and it has nothing to do with age.

This book again takes a refreshing look at what's right with age. No pills or potions, just true-life examples of extraordinary aging which offer hope, insight, and inspiration for what's possible with age by learning what's worked for others. With a combination of more SuperSenior stories, along with two new sections on celebrities and 'Life Lessons' (addressing a variety of aging issues), there's definitely a right way to do age in a healthy, happy way, and this book shares the secrets of those who have.

These stories feature humble people. They don't want to brag or boast, nor do they think that what they are doing is extraordinary. They do what they do because they enjoy it, and it makes them feel good mentally, physically, and soulfully. If their stories and experiences can help change beliefs and mindsets about what's possible with age or encourage and motivate others to feel good too, then perhaps this book will serve as a valuable tool to create a new style of positive, healthy aging for years to come and help to forever change the way we age.

It's time to share the secrets of aging well, related by those who are actually doing it. Call them secrets, or perhaps choices these people made in order to age well. There are definite similarities, but each individual also has a personal story that makes their journey unique. By experiencing the adventures taken by others, perhaps this book will inspire an adventure in you and forever change the way you age, too!

There is no specific order to the book ... open it up to any page, at any time, and you will be inspired. The only rule is: Never let age get in the way of life!

Letter to the Reader
ॐ

On the journey of life, the road offers different paths . . . the choices we make often determine our direction and destination. Yet we all desire to travel the path of good health and happiness with a zest for life and a feeling of fulfillment each new day, regardless of our age.

This book provides a road map for an adventure; it reveals how others have found this destination, a place where age is just a number and few feel their actual age. It is a place where age and life are celebrated, instilling a feeling of hope about what's possible. It's an attainable destination to us all . . . the destination is within ourselves.

The secrets to aging well lie within these pages: words of wisdom gained from experience, which are applicable and enlightening to us all. Enchanting, engaging, inspiring, and fun . . . they teach us to always enjoy life's journey!

Love, Health, and happiness always,

The Age Angel

LIFE LESSONS

&

Ageless State of Mind

ह

There are few greater feelings than being inspired and motivated. Regardless of what or who it is, or what we do that makes us tick -- it's important to feel positive and enthusiastic about life. Look for the good news in life and see how much better you may feel as a result.

The attitude of gratitude, being appreciative for the many blessings we have in our lives is a wonderful way to start. Certainly there will always be changes and challenges along the way, but to move on and forge forward leaving the negative behind has proven to be one of the key components in maintaining well being late in life.

Working in the field of aging is truly one of the most rewarding and fulfilling things I believe I could ever be involved in. Some find it strange perhaps, that at a time in life where losses and decline are seemingly inevitable, how could that be? However, what being with seniors, or the "wisdom keepers," has taught me (which the research also confirms), is that it's what's deep inside us that really matters -- what we think and what we feel can be ageless.

Some may think I'm referring to agelessness as being young. Nope, that's not what I mean. What really matters is being accepting of who we are, with all the changes and challenges we've experienced along the way, and knowing that each of these life situations has contributed to who we are today.

1

People are always fascinated by centenarians (those people living to the age of 100), and are often intrigued by what it takes to live that long. Studies show that while genetics and exercise certainly play a role, anew key component is their ability to manage stress -- their ability to roll with the punches.

Living to 100, just in itself, would likely seem to give you a lot of practice at doing this, but I believe it takes one more key ingredient, morale. You've got to feel good about yourself, your fellow man, and life itself; otherwise it's a losing battle. You've got to have faith that good things will come. If you believe, you will achieve and all those other clichés can be powerful words when used in the right context and applied to our lives.

I'm inspired daily in my work and study on aging, from the actual seniors themselves to the research and professionals in this field. Of particular interest are the varied views of one's aging experience. There are those who feel and seem ancient at 40, and others who are vibrant and vital even at 80. Countless others don't even feel or think about their age -- not that they feel either young or old, or even middle age, but rather ageless -- believing age is just a number.

This is a good thing because much of the aging research today recognizes that it is the psychological age -- how old we feel, that is far more important and influential in determining how our aging years will be than the chronological age -- how old we actually are.

But where does that come from and how can we all have that feeling? There is no magic pill or potion, but the good news is -- it comes from within. Deep inside each of us is a spirit of being. It's not necessarily about becoming something different, but more like a state of pure being that never ages, has no age and therefore is ageless.

While some may confuse this with an effort to be younger, it's really about finding our "true being." It is at this place and in this state where instead of getting older and aging, we actually become ageless -- a person without age, who lives life without worrying about how old they are and instead lives all the days of their life.

Centenarian Secrets

&

C an you believe that one in three girls born today will see their 100th birthday? It's true! And it's even projected that one in twenty baby boomers may put 100 candles on their birthday cakes, too. As we live longer, healthier lives, we're learning more about the secrets of what it actually takes to become a centenarian.

There are currently 65,000 centenarians in the United States. That's four-times what we had just ten years ago and the numbers are expected to double within the next ten years, so the growth is also happening at a very quick rate. In fact, the 85+ age group is the fastest growing segment of our population today.

I've had the privilege and pleasure to talk with a number of centenarians and my favorite story is Jeanne Calment of France, the oldest person in the world, who lived to 122, documented. She was simply amazing -- didn't even stop smoking and drinking until the age of 117! But she was very active, healthy and loved life, which undoubtedly contributed to her extraordinary longevity.

According to Tom Perls, M.D., MPH, and Director of the New England Centenarian Study at Boston Medical School, who started his study in 1994 with 800 participants, there are definite similarities among those living a century or more.

"The majority of centenarians are women, obviously, since women live longer than men," Perls stated. "Only 15% of centenarians are men and even though we have more centenarians than ever before, you'll still only find about one per 10,000 people," Perls reported.

Rarer yet is to find what Perls identifies as "super centenarians" defined as 100-year old married couples, which occurs in only one of every ten million people. Perls actually met one such couple and will never forget the fact that the husband's secret to longevity was putting olive oil on his cereal!

The interesting thing is that while 70% of the aging process is based on lifestyle and 30% on genetics (according to a Mt. Sinai Medical Center in New York study), living to the age of 100 is seemingly more genetically driven.

Studies on centenarians show that if a sibling reaches the age of 100, brothers of that sibling have a 17-time greater chance of living to 100 and sisters have an 8-time greater chance. One family studied had five of nine siblings reach the age of 100.

The reality however, is you've got to get to the age of 70 or 80 first, and although genetics play a role in living to 100, environment and lifestyle choices play a more prominent role in reaching the earlier ages. "Reaching the age of 70 and 80 is very much in our control," Perls stated. "Most people have been given a terrific poker hand that should enable them to live to the late 80s. But what inevitably happens is the result of poor lifestyle choices, which cause the health problems that generally ends the journey for most, earlier than later."

While it's no secret that keeping active, contributing, staying involved, lifelong learning, having humor, friends, and faith, combined with healthy living, increase your odds of experiencing a good, quality of life at all ages -- it's most essential in increasing your chances of being a centenarian because you've got to get to the age of 80 in good health first!

So what can we do now to increase our odds of experiencing this amazing feat of longevity? According to researchers at Harvard Medical School who have also specifically studied centenarians, there are simple steps we can take, regardless of age, that can help minimize poor health and major disabilities later in life.

First and foremost, maintain a positive attitude and lighten your emotional load. Negative thinking and stress can take a toll on our health so it's important to learn how to let go of what can't be changed, adapt and take control of the aspects in life you can influence.

That leads us to another factor, learning to eat and drink healthily and in moderation. Weight gain can be the beginning of a number of health problems ranging from diabetes to joint problems. I've yet to meet an overweight centenarian. And alcohol is also rarely consumed by most centenarians -- certainly in moderation, if at all.

Challenging our brain is equally important, so by continuing to perform brain-boosting activities like learning new things, crossword puzzles, etc, this helps with the growth of new dendrites in the brain, which compensates for some of the deterioration that is an inevitable aspect of aging.

Keeping in touch with friends and family and the importance of personal relationships are also important factors. People need people, and those with social contacts often age well. From volunteering to just having someone to laugh, cry or sigh with makes life worth living.

Finally, make activity a daily part of your life. It does-n't necessarily have to be formal exercise, but just moving your body every day keeps you healthy and less susceptible to health hiccups along the way. Walking and climbing stairs are some of the best activities since they help improve balance and muscle strength, which decreases the risk of falls - one of the leading causes of death in older people.

As more and more people recognize the role they play in their own longevity, we'll likely continue making great strides in living long.

I wonder if the birthday candle industry has started mass production of their product because it looks like lots of candles might be needed on future birthday cakes!

Functional Fitness Prevents Falls

೮౨

F unctional Fitness is one of the hottest trends in exercise and aging, due to the focus on exercises that improve ones ability to perform the activities of daily living. This is not just your typical exercise class -- these are specific exercises designed to help people maintain their independence, which is an important issue among older adults today.

Research currently shows that the primary determinant for admission to a nursing home is loss of functional capacity -- much of which is due to loss of muscle mass, which often then results in frailty, fractures, and disability. But with the proper type of exercise program, much of this loss can be stopped, and even reversed.

"I'm absolutely amazed at how much stronger I feel and what a difference it's made in my daily activities," Phyllis shared. "I used to have to use a walker in the morning to help pull me up out of bed. Not anymore. My legs are so much stronger -- actually it's not just my legs, my arms, my whole body feels stronger, so I've put the walker away because I don't need it now!"

Preserving balance and flexibility is one of the most important things you can do to maintain your independence and good health with age. Exercise designed to help people increase their strength, stability, and flexibility, ultimately works to reduce one's risk of falling, which is a serious problem with age because almost 30% of all people over age 65 suffer falls each year, and about half of these falls cause serious injuries. Plus, the risk only worsens with age; about 50% of all people over 80 fall each year. Additionally, older adults who fall are three times more likely to require nursing home care than their contemporaries who don't suffer a fall. Plus, serious falls that lead to broken hips or other major injuries are a leading cause of death in older people.

I've long been a believer of prevention and now that we know how to help people lessen their risk of falling, it's important to provide these types of programs in the community. But in many ways, these types of programs do more that just help people improve their physical abilities -- it also helps improve confidence, plus participants equally enjoy the social benefits.

"It's great to be around other people who are interested in helping themselves feel better and are actually doing something about it," said one class member who wanted to remain anonymous." "It's really quite inspiring to see the range of improvements we've all made and it's nice to have a group of new friends to share this good news and experience with."

According to an analysis of the cause of falls, published in the American Family Physician, half of falls by older adults are accidents -- such as falling on a slippery floor, while the other half are the result of physical weakness, gait problems, or the effects of drugs or illness.

While Functional Fitness programs definitely address improving physical weakness and gait problems, there's another significant issue: having confidence that you won't suffer a fall. This is a much bigger issue with people than you might think because what happens more times than not is a person will restrict their activities to guard against the potential of falling. When people are afraid of falling they stop doing things altogether, which then results in loss of muscle strength from inactivity, as well as isolation -- which can then lead to emotional problems like depression.

It's interesting to see the connection between physical and emotional, and even more exciting to know there are things we can do to improve our quality of life.

Future Health Care Requires Self Reliance
&

W hen the Declaration of Independence was signed in
1776, the average life expectancy was 35 years
old. Imagine living in a time when most people
were dead by their thirty-fifth birthday. Through the extraordinary breakthroughs in healthcare, we've basically eliminated
the diseases that killed people at early ages which have contributed to our increased life expectancy today.

But where are we headed? With the projected aging of
America and a healthcare system already on the verge of collapse, will things get worse before they get better and what is
our role in the process?

The breakthroughs of the 20th century increased life
expectancy an astounding 30 years. We've increased life
expectancy more in the last century than the entire previous
time in history. The early years of the 21st century are
expected to be like no previous age in history, resulting in 40
to 50 million Americans over the age of 65, and most destined
to live well into their 80s. It's even possible that life
expectancy will hit 90, adding an amazing twelve years to
today's already impressive 78 years of life for the average
human being.

So yes, we're all living longer lives and this trend will
likely continue. Yet while the majority of us will live longer,
healthier, vital lives, there will still be a percentage of older

adults who will experience increasing health challenges. Although this is only a small minority of our aging population today, (only 5% of the 65+ population is institutionalized) the numbers and costs will likely continue to rise. It is already estimated that the sickest 10% of Medicare patients account for 75% of Medicare expenses. So with most Americans living into their 80s, if old age health does not improve from today's levels, the economy will be faced with tremendous pressure.

What will happen to our already crumbling health care system if we continue doing things the same way and the avalanche of expected consumers continues to head its way?

According to Dr. Dean Schneider, head of the Andrus Gerontology Center at USC, if elder health improves, future 85-year olds will have the vigor of today's 70-year olds with modest needs for medical care and the ability to lead full and active lives. But if health does not improve from today's levels, the economy will be burdened with special needs for nursing care, transportation, housing and medical arrangements.

Currently less than 1% of the $1.14 trillion the U.S. spends each year on health care goes for research on Alzheimer's, Arthritis, Parkinson's, Prostate Cancer and other diseases that debilitate older people. Yet finding cures for these diseases could have a huge positive effect on the economy.

At the Milken Institute, a Santa Monica-based think-tank, an investment of $175 million in diabetes research now saves $7 billion in medical costs. The economic value of reductions in heart disease in people aged 70 to 80 mounts to $15 trillion.

It's obvious we definitely, and desperately need new direction in federal expenditures for Medicare and other pro-

grams. Unless more diseases of aging are delayed or con-
quered, mounting medical bills will swamp even the most
robust Medicare program -- and our Medicare program is anything but "robust."

And what about individual economics? Are people
making the important connection between health and wealth --
that the healthier you are, the wealthier you'll be due to spending less on health care?

Self-reliance and self-responsibility for health is a
must for this century. Life is what we make of it. And
although this way of thinking may seem too simplistic for
some, I believe, and have seen it achieved, that this is the right
place to start for most.

Rather than looking for the next quick fix or the
"youth pill" of tomorrow, current longevity studies indicate
that 70% of the characteristics of aging are lifestyle-related,
while only 30% are based on genetics. We need to recognize
the role we, as individuals, play in our own aging process. Of
the 10 leading health problems for people 65+, 80% are
lifestyle related, meaning they are not automatic, inevitable
aspects of aging. It's high time we start paying attention to
these facts.

According to most, it's not how long one lives, but
rather how well. It's quality of life we're after and health generally plays an essential role in the process. But before
lifestyle changes can be made, people need to change their
attitude, mindset and beliefs about what's possible in the second half of life. If we believe our later years can be a time of
good health, vitality, and productivity, then we're more likely
to incorporate the lifestyle behaviors that will enable that to
happen. On the other hand, if we believe aging is an automatic time of decline, we're undoubtedly less likely to take care
of ourselves -- and the result will be a self-fulfilling prophecy.

With all the remarkable accomplishments and break-throughs anticipated for the 21st century, a new dawning for aging is possible. But it won't happen without a change in thinking and behavior among society as a whole. We, as individuals, must also do our part by making healthy lifestyle choices and taking more responsibility for our own health. It is not the health care system's job to take care of us, it's our job to take care of us and only then will we benefit from all this new longevity has to offer.

Give to Live

৶

People are genuinely intrigued with the study of aging, gerontology and the prospect of living longer. So it should come as no surprise that as a gerontologist, I am constantly quizzed about the 'secrets' to living a long and healthy life.

There are numerous theories regarding the steps people can take to ensure a healthy lifespan, however, what about our quality of life? Everyone's so caught up with how old they are and looking for ways to slow down the aging process that we seem to forget about more meaningful, humanistic elements.

I can't help but think what a different world it would be if people, of all ages frankly, would pay more attention to having meaning in their life instead of focusing just on how to stay younger. What's the point in extending life if you're not making a difference in the world? If you think it's all about staying young, you're in for a big surprise -- and undoubtedly some disappointment.

One can certainly strive toward being healthy, vital, and productive throughout their life -- those are ageless qualities that can enable us to feel younger and even continue to contribute longer. Perhaps that's what we really should be paying more attention to: the things we can do that will make us feel better about ourselves and our lives because ultimately, these elements will make a difference to others and our world too.

I've read countless articles, consumed many research briefs, and conducted hundreds of personal interviews in search of uncovering the most important, innovative issues that enable people to age well. I continue to come back to the same answer -- ultimately, it comes from within. In many ways, it's how we feel about ourselves and that which we give of ourselves that really measures how 'well' we are physically, emotionally, and mentally. Rarely does it have anything to do with age, other than the fact that as we grow older, our emphasis on what's important seems to shift a bit as we get beyond the coming and goings of middle-age survival mode and come into a time when we can be more reflective of life's real meaning.

One consistency I've discovered among those who claim they are 'aging well' has been their commitment to making a difference in someone else's life. Some have experienced a direct impact in a one-on-one basis, others are involved in programs where they don't see the result of their efforts directly, but knowing they're making a difference is just as beneficial. There are others who have coincidentally uncovered the tremendous benefits of giving by going through their own difficult grief or healing process and tell how focusing their attention on helping someone else, greatly lessened their own burden.

So next time you're looking for a way to improve your life, reach out and help someone else because 'Give to Live' is the real deal and what a wonderful world it would be if we all really did.

Happy-Ology

&

I recently gave a talk on "Happy-Ology," and was absolutely amazed at the interest it generated. Seems there's plenty of research and information about how to live long, but if we're not happy -- who cares how long we live. While some may feel a bit vague on this "happiness" thing, studies show that we better start figuring it out because it has a direct affect on our health.

Why is it that people seem to have such difficulty with the things we can't see or touch, like the intangibles of emotions? Everyone wants to be happy but why haven't we figured out that it's up to us? It really is an internal mechanism we control just like other aspects of our lives. Of course, when you have cosmetic companies like Clinique selling "Happy" in a bottle as a type of perfume, perhaps that's why there's some confusion. The advertising campaign convinces us to just spray it on -- and presto, we'll be happy!

I love the saying, "the most important things in life are free," because it's true. The challenge however, is maintaining that perspective in a society that continually barrages us with a belief that consumerism and materialism is what it's all about. But what happens when you've done all that and discover that you're still not fulfilled . . . let alone, happy? And particularly in regards to aging, there are some who don't even think you can be happy as you grow older because of all the experiences with changes and losses. Then there are others who say retirement is absolutely the best time of their life.

Regardless of what stage or age you are in life, we are fascinated with concept of happiness. I recently attended a "Humor and Laughter" lecture on the neuroimmunology of humor (humor's effect on the immune system) and it's evident that this silliness is really serious stuff.

Drs. David Feldon and Lee Berk, directors of the Center for Neuroimmunology at Loma Linda University, were the guest speakers and their research concludes that there indeed is a connection to what we think and how we feel. Amazingly, however, is the reality that even with all the extraordinary breakthroughs we've experienced in healthcare through the 20th century, we're still relatively primitive in our understanding of the effect our emotions have on our physical health.

I'm convinced now more than ever that this must be due to the difficulty of measuring and accurately quantifying these aspects, because the results clearly speak for themselves. It's a challenge to "prove" scientifically, that emotional intangibles do directly affect our life, and as a result, perhaps that's why we're so curious about this thing called happiness.

The research science of laughter definitely concludes that it does work as an agent on the immune system by increasing the number of natural killer cells. The initial study in the 1980s by the late Dr. Norman Cousins, who experimented with his own cancer diagnosis by watching reruns of Candid Camera and Laurel & Hardy comedy routines, concluded that laughter helped him heal and that the only time he felt good was when we was laughing. Dr. Cousins opened the door to explore the connection more thoroughly by recruiting Dr. Berk, who has since continued to conduct this research, which has resulted in the scientific proof that there is a valid link.

It's nice to know that science is finally catching up with intuition. Most people do believe there is a mind/body connection -- that what we think and feel does affect how we are physically. Now there's actual scientific proof that it's true.

So go out and get happy because as we grow older studies also clearly show we're simply not smiling and laughing as much as we perhaps should. Did you know that children laugh an average of 400 times a day; and adults average only 15?

So next time you get a prescription from your doctor to rest, drink more fluids, and take a couple aspirin, be sure to add a cup of laughter to your day, too!

Health Concerns Target Diabetes & Obesity
ৎ৩

Recently there's been an abundance of health related facts in the press that raise real concern. Particularly the increase in diabetes and obesity, which is at an all-time high for people of all ages, resulting in a variety of serious health and lifestyle problems that for the most part are preventable.

A recent ABC news report stated that the medical costs for treating conditions associated with obesity is more than the costs for health problems caused from tobacco and alcohol combined.

Obesity has been rising steadily since 1991 and is actually gaining on tobacco as the leading cause of preventable death. According to the Center for Disease Control (CDC), currently about 60% of U.S. adults and 13% of children are overweight and more than 300K people die each year from illnesses caused or made worse by obesity.

So what happened in America -- did we put down the cigarettes and pick up a fork? It's a possibility certainly, but it's doesn't explain the reason for the increase of obesity in children. In fact, one of the most frightening statistics I've ever read is that we're actually seeing the diagnosis of age-related health conditions like osteoporosis and diabetes 2 in our youth! This is a definite lifestyle issue -- likely an increase in high fat/sugar diets and a decrease in exercise and activity.

As adults, we recognize the importance of healthy lifestyle choices, but for some reason we still blame many of the health problems we incur later in life on age. But when you see the increase of these problems in children now too, can we really blame this on age? The CDC also reports the number of people in their 30s with type 2 diabetes has increased 70%, while the increase among children has increased tenfold in the past 5 years. That's an epidemic and a definite healthcare crisis coming down the pike.

The association between an increase and obesity and an increase in diabetes is a no-brainer. Genetics account for only 15-20% of diabetes. The real culprit is our high-fat, high-stress, no-time-for-exercise way of life and the epidemic of obesity that comes with that. Studies show that obesity raises diabetes risk by up to a whopping 93%. Inactivity alone, raises the risk by 25%.

So what's the answer? Eat less and move more. Pretty simple. And as Jack LaLanne says, "We're exceeding the feed limit!"

Granted, there are some biological and physiological reasons as to why weight gain becomes more common with age. Somewhere in our 30s, our metabolism starts to slow down by about 1% per year -- or 10% per decade. So if you ate 1,800 calories a day and fit into a size 10 in your 30s, you'll be shopping for size 12s in your 40s -- even if you're eating the same number of calories. By the time you're 55 -- well, you get the idea.

The culprit behind the decline in calorie-burn is largely due to muscle loss. Starting in our 50s we lose about a 1/2 lb of muscle per year - a loss that often doubles during the menopause years. And with every pound of muscle you lose, it decreases the number of calories you burn. So by the time we reach 65, it's possible to have lost HALF of our muscle mass and therefore see our metabolism slowed by 200-300 calories a day! Result: weight gain.

But even with all these physiological reasons, we can still reverse and/or slow down these losses by getting fit. There's that word again -- exercise, activity, move it or lose it. But it's true! Specifically, lifting lightweights is one of the best remedies. In a recent study of sedentary people in their 60s and 70s who strength trained 3x a week for 6 months, they increased their daily calorie burn by more than 230 calories! One third of that increase alone, was due to a boost in their metabolism from muscle gain. Regardless of age, muscle can be re-attained.

Whether you have diabetes or not, are overweight or not, the benefits one can achieve through regular exercise is worth a try. You think better, eat better, move better, feel better, lessen the likelihood of health problems, and the costs that come with them.

Intergenerational Games

&

Crossing Generations

D o we ever get to a stage in life when role models are no longer important? Most all of us likely remember certain people in our lives who served as an example, taught us life lessons, or were just always there for us providing some sort of support or guidance. But what is it like to actually be a role model? Did you know that most of you probably are, but may not even realize it?

I recently had the opportunity to both observe and participate in the first annual Intergenerational Games held at the U.S. Olympic Training Center, which brought together local 4th grade students and older adult athletes from the Senior Olympics for a day of fun activity and interaction between generations, using sport and physical activity as the link.

Over 50 student and senior partner teams spent the day together navigating their way through a variety of skill and knowledge challenges, ranging from a basketball toss to local sports trivia questions, all designed with an emphasis more on fun than competition.

One of the main objectives of this event was the hope that by linking senior athletes and students together, kids would learn the importance and fun of being healthy all through life, and that you're never too old to play and have fun!

Additionally important was the issue of stereotyping. Rarely do young people view older adults in a positive light, but it's usually just a matter of having the opportunity to connect and perhaps see people in a different way.

"Some kids don't even have an older adult or grandparent as a role model at all, so by partnering kids and seniors together, this gave us the opportunity to broaden everyone's perspective a bit," said Katie Judd, event coordinator. "Seniors today are no longer retiring to the easy chair. They want to keep active, stay healthy, and be involved, so this event was a great way to link generations together, and hopefully diminish stereotyping, while also learning from each other."

Embracing and celebrating all aspects of aging is not just a nice thing to do, but necessary. Generating positive awareness between generations may even help facilitate a reduction in youth violence and even foster improved family support.

Of course, one of the issues of great concern today is the lack of physical activity opportunities available to our youth within the school system. Budget cuts have pretty well eliminated exercise and activity from the curriculum, which unfortunately has now created a whole new set of health problems among our young adults.

The Center for Disease Control (CDC) reports that the number of people with Diabetes 2 (known as Adult Onset Diabetes because it has historically been diagnosed exclusively in older people) has increased 70 percent among people in their 30s, and the increase among children has increased ten-fold in the last five years! This is an epidemic and a definite healthcare crisis coming down the pike that will unlikely cost considerably more to treat than any savings being made by cutting these types of programs.

With one of the goals of this first annual Intergenerational Games being to increase mutual understanding and respect between generations and to promote healthy, active, life-long behaviors, it's evident that not only was this achieved, but more importantly, really needed.

"I've never played sports with my Grandma before," said one student. "I didn't even think Grandmas could do this stuff, but they can and that's cool!"

Changing people's mindsets about what's possible, particularly with age, is one of the most positive things we can do in this society. Imagine the contributions that could be made if people believed they still had something to contribute, regardless of their age, and the effect it would have on others of all ages.

At this inaugural event, although scores were kept and medals awarded, everyone was a winner. During the award ceremony it was obvious this goal had been achieved as one student participant whispered to her new senior friend, "It doesn't matter if you win or lose, it's how you play the game!"

We're all role models and mentors in our own way, because as humans, we're always watching and learning from each other. So it's not only about how you play the game -- it's about playing it period, at every age. And more importantly, may we all remember that we don't stop playing because we get old -- we get old because we stop playing.

Jack LaLanne

ℰℴ

Exudes Vitality

I
f you are interested in learning more about how you can incorporate vitality into your life, there may be no one on the planet better to emulate than Jack LaLanne!

Yes, Jack LaLanne is alive and well -- likely in better shape than people half his age!

In fact, just a few years ago, Jack was asked to participate in a national study by Fitness Age, a company who had designed a series of physical tests individuals could take to measure their physiological age, or personal "fitness" age to determine how it differed from their actual chronological age. No surprise -- Jack's results were equally as impressive as the man. At the age of 86, Jack LaLanne had the physiological make-up or "fitness age" of a 29-year old!

Yes, that's right, Jack LaLanne is exemplary of good health and coincidentally, has few of the age-related aches, pains, and other health problems typically seen in people his age. There's obviously a connection between lifestyle and the aging process, and people of all ages need to be aware of just how much control we really do have over how long and how well we live, and what steps to take to be happy and healthy, as well as vital, regardless of age.

One of the first steps is to get rid of the negative stereotype and mindset we have about getting older. Maintaining a positive outlook can greatly determine how well we age. If we believe we actually do have some control over our aging process, think how much differently we might live our lives. We'd likely be more apt to take an ACTIVE role in our lives by incorporating the lifestyle behaviors that would make a difference. On the other hand, if we believe our later years are automatically going to be a time of decline and poor health, than why bother taking care of ourselves with healthy lifestyle choices if we don't think it will matter anyway.

This is probably one of the most exciting and powerful issues facing aging today -- that there are definitely simple things we can do on a daily basis that contribute to improving our quality of life -- not to mention the added bonus of increasing our health span, too. I've never believed we should focus on just living as long as humanly possible, but rather as WELL as possible. And if we're all getting older and living longer, doesn't it make sense to help people learn how to do it in a healthy, happy way?

Some of the current long-term studies on aging state that 70% is based on lifestyle, while only 30% on genetics! That's huge! Most people actually think it's the opposite -- that genetics play a larger role than lifestyle. This is great news because what this means is that what we do on a day-to-day basis can affect not only how long we live, but more importantly, how well we live -- and that's what really counts.

Jack LaLanne has always been THE man when people think of fitness. He's the 'Godfather of Fitness'. But there was a time many of you probably remember when Jack was considered a fruitcake -- people thought he was absolutely nuts preaching the benefits of fitness. My how things change. Today, Jack is actually considered a "visionary" for his

remarkable insight into the benefits of exercise. He's a walking billboard for healthy aging and there's no one who can tell
the story better than Jack.

Of course, Jack has an amazing tale to tell and he's
certainly been creative in his ability to generate excitement in
sharing the healthy aging message. His "feats" have been
extraordinary since starting at age 40, when he swam the
entire length of the Golden Gate Bridge underwater with 140
pounds of equipment, and at 70, he towed 70 boats filled with
70 people for 1 1/2 miles, while handcuffed and shackled.
Even in his 80s, Jack continued to delight people with his fitness antics by swimming from Catalina Island to Los Angeles!
And at 90, he wants to swim underwater with tanks, from
Long Beach to Catalina.

"I believe in my profession more now than I ever have
in my whole life," declares Jack LaLanne, who maintains an
amazing amount of boundless energy. "I've never been more
enthusiastic about my life than I am today. In fact, when I die
it's going to ruin my image," he joked.

While Jack continues to exemplify the tremendous
importance of exercise all the way through life, it certainly
isn't the only thing one needs to do to remain vital later in life.
The "use it or lose it" philosophy applies not only to getting
daily physical activity, but it's also important to keep the brain
active and mentally fit. Additionally, the importance of being
involved in activities you enjoy, trying new things, staying
connected with people rather than isolating oneself, and maintaining a positive spirit and attitude are all essential aspects of
vitality -- regardless of age.

Life According to Linkletter

ℬ

Speaking to a standing-room only crowd -- after a standing ovation welcome, Art Linkletter exuberantly stated in his opening remarks, "I'm having the time of my life!" And if humor, contribution, and lifelong learning are indeed among the key components to living a healthy, long life -- Art Linkletter is on an incredible journey.

Linkletter has that "joie-de-vivre" (joy of life) and ageless spirit that makes him a pure delight to be around. Granted, he is a celebrity, famous-type person who has achieved great success, but I'd bet that if you took it all away from him tomorrow, he'd still be a remarkable, engaged individual who would continue to make a positive difference in the world.

His 30+ year career in the entertainment industry started in the 1930s as a radio announcer, yet he is most often recognized and still remembered as the host of his widely popular, "Kids Say the Darndest Things" television series.

One of his favorite examples of kids telling it like it is was with his own great grandson who asked him to speak at his school. He introduced him in that typical, kid-classic, honest-humor style by saying, "This is my Grandfather -- he's 80 and still alive!"

Linkletter is most definitely alive -- still active and living life. He's involved in a variety of business ventures ranging from solar power (in which he's considered one of the leading experts), and a variety of entrepreneurial enterprises, while also serving on the Board of a number of prestigious organizations. He obviously believes very strongly in the importance and value of staying involved in meaningful activities throughout life as one of the secrets to living a healthy, long life -- and he's certainly practicing what he preaches.

"I'm happy to be living and learning new things at every age and stage along the way," Art said. "Having a challenge and purpose in life is so important -- and being able to enjoy the wisdom that can only be acquired through life experiences, is certainly one of the benefits that comes with age."

As you might expect, in addition to sprinkling his talk with nuggets of wisdom -- humor plays an important part too. "Life is what happens to you when you're making plans," he shared. "Phyllis Diller once told me that if you really want to make God laugh, tell him your plans!"

A sense of humor we know is an important trait in getting through life. Linkletter says he feels blessed to have recognized early on that sometimes the simplest things in life can actually be the most humorous, which likely explains the success theory behind his long-running television series.

"In addition to laughter being fun to do, it makes you feel good too," Linkletter said. "Scientists have determined that beneficial, physical things actually occur in our bodies when we laugh. We release endorphins that do all sorts of good things for us. So get out there and look for the funny things in life!"

But when Linkletter talks about what makes people happy in life, he's quick to point out that it's not about money, power, and fame. He believes it's in the importance of learning and having a purpose.

"We need to encourage older adults to continue growing, learning, and experiencing new things in order to enjoy
the most life has to offer," Art said. "The value of adult education is one of the best things we can encourage people to do."

Linkletter also believes in a basic motto, "Make the
best of the rest of your life." And although he's often referred
to as the Ambassador for Positive Living, it hasn't always
been easy. In fact, it was actually a personal tragedy thirty
years ago that brought him to where he is today.

"One of the most difficult days of my life was receiv-
ing the news that my 20-year old daughter had committed sui-
cide experimenting with LSD," Art sadly remembered. "Right
then and there, that very day, I quit my TV work and chose to
try and help others faced with similar tragedy. I quickly
became a public voice in the crusade against drugs."

On this mission, Linkletter spoke at the White House,
United Nations and many other venues to help fight drug
abuse. And it was during this work that he discovered his love
for talking about issues people really cared about in order to
help make a difference. He lectured everywhere from prisons
to boardrooms, all in an effort to help prevent other families
from suffering, too.

Today, Art is still a man on a mission -- continuing to
make a positive difference in the world. And with his wife of
67 years, Lois, by his side, along with his nine grandchildren
and fourteen great-grandchildren, he's vowed to continue
growing -- "growing up," that is.

"Getting older means different things to different people," Art said. "It's not how old you are, it's how are you, old.
The key is to never stop growing. Maintain the childlike won-
ders of lifelong learning and exploration and you too, will
have the time of your life!"

Live Long, Live Strong

ɞ

B elieve me when I tell you, it's an exciting time to be
growing older. Don't laugh, I'm serious. Aging is
definitely "in" -- it's hip, it's cool, it's the buzz, the
rage, and everybody's talking about it because everybody's
doing it! The key now however, seems to be how we each
choose to age, and that undoubtedly, is what has everybody
talking.

If you're like most, you probably don't believe you
have much control over how you age. But according to the
information presented recently at the American College of
Sports Medicine's (ACSM) national conference, not only do
we play a major role -- now there's research to back it up.

In the twenty-plus years I've spent in this field, I've yet
to meet one older adult who doesn't tell me that maintaining
their health and independence are two of the most important
things in their life. And the two go hand-in-hand. Without
your health, you risk losing your independence. It's not about
how long we live, it's about how well we live -- the quality of
life is what really matters. And I've always believed that
health is best defined as the capacity an individual has to do
what he or she wants to do. That, to me, is living.

But the reality is, it's our choice. We can no longer
continue to blame all our problems on age. How we live our
lives today influences both our longevity and our chances of

disability -- and never before has the research been so strong in support of this reality. The best news however, is it's never too late to incorporate healthy lifestyles and benefit. You're never too old to make changes, but ultimately the choice is still yours.

Consider the facts: Fifty-percent of women and thirty-percent of men over 65 can't cross the street before the traffic light changes, nor lift a ten-pound bag of groceries. And as people get older, these statistics become even more frightening. Studies from Tufts University show we lose between one-third to one-half a pound of muscle each year starting at age 30, and generally replace it with a minimum of one pound of fat.

Additionally, inactivity seems to accompany aging, which means these physiological changes are only half the story. "Sarcopenia" is a term coined by Dr. Rosenberg (Tufts University) to describe the additional loss of muscle mass that occurs exclusively with inactivity. The combination of the two results in frailty, disability, fractures, and/or numerous other health problems that often then require institutionalization -- a loss of one's independence due to the inability to perform the activities of daily living.

Studies today however, are showing that much of this is preventable. Aging is a cumulative process, not an overnight occurrence. So instead of just accepting this decline, research is focusing on ways to challenge late life frailty and the results are clearly exciting. Part of the excitement is due not only to the dramatic improvements older adults experience, but more importantly, few are immune to reversing the changes that once were just accepted as inevitable decline.

The hottest thing going right now is "functional fitness," which basically means performing exercises that

improve the aspects of daily living. There's a big difference
between doing specific types of exercises for the purpose of
maintaining ones independence versus exercising just because
it's suppose to be good for you. Particularly when the
research now shows that the primary determinant for admission to a nursing home is loss of functional capacity. If we
have some control over that happening, we're talking about a
significant difference in a person's quality of life.

Although this is among the most innovative, break-
through research in the field of aging, there's still an outdated
belief among many people (including some physicians not
current on the latest findings) who believe exercise -- particularly strength training workouts with lightweights, is bad for
older adults. The belief that muscle loss, resulting in frailty
and disability, is just inevitable. Wrong. Studies done even
among the frailest elderly population already in nursing
homes, show that they too can double, triple, and even
quadruple muscle strength in their 70s, 80s, 90s, and even
100s, and benefit with increased self-sufficiency like getting
out of a chair by themselves, or walking without an aid. Let
alone the improvements seen by those more independent older
adults who also showed increases in strength which made
activities easier and more enjoyable, who experienced significant reductions in joint pain, decreased risk of falling,
improved sense of balance, better sleep patterns, less depression, and the list goes on and on and on.

Probably the most famous research done in this area
has been by Dr. Miriam Nelson, author of *Strong Women Stay
Young*, *Strong Women Stay Slim*, and *Strong Women, Strong
Bones*. Don't be fooled into thinking this is just a women's
subject because the facts are equal for men. In fact Nelson's
latest book address this issue specifically with men.

This is exciting information and there's more and more
research addressing this issue. So get serious about getting
strong and just do it! Remember, it's your life so live strong.

41

Love Is Ageless

&

W hy does everyone seem to think age changes people? Sure, it may affect our physical abilities and
appearances, but it doesn't change who we are and
how we feel on the inside. And isn't that what really matters
most anyway?

One of the "hot" topics I'm continually asked about is
love later in life. First and foremost, love is ageless. We're
never too old to fall in love, and the desire for companionship,
and sharing life with another, or having someone to care about
is part of being human -- it has nothing to do with age.

The reality, however with aging, is that as we grow
older, we do lose loved ones and therefore it's fairly common
to experience the "single senior stage". But that doesn't mean
you're not capable of or interested in love, or in having a partner and friend to continue life with. Often the real challenge
is getting over the mental block or stereotype that says you're
too old to even be thinking about this -- or for our family or
friends to get over it, which often times is where this problem
starts.

I'm always intrigued by the role reversal that often
takes place with age -- where the children become the parents,
and the parents are often treated like children. Certainly I recognize that as we get older we sometimes do need assistance
with a variety of things, but to think that an older adult isn't

able to make certain emotional decisions, or that because they've fallen in love late in life, they must be senile, is flat out wrong! Granted, most are only trying to protect their parents from making a bad decision or getting hurt . . . or perhaps even protecting their own inheritance can also be an issue. But to believe that love and/or intimate relationships are not important, or possible at this stage of life, is not allowing one to live life to the fullest, regardless of age.

I've been fortunate enough in my work to interact with literally hundreds of older adults and therefore have seen quite an array of relationship situations. There are the inspiring tales of two who are fortunate enough to celebrate 50th wedding anniversaries, and even those who celebrate 60th and beyond. There are others who lose the love of their life and never seem to recover. To varying degrees and in different ways, they continue to suffer their loss and hold back from ever fully opening their hearts again. Then there are those who feel like something's missing in their lives, or perhaps by happen chance, discover someone that makes them smile inside and seek out the opportunity to fill the empty void.

Regardless of the situation, the reality is love -- and the joy that comes from caring for someone else, or being cared about, is an essential aspect of life. There are as many ways to experience love, as there are people -- and no one way is the only way. Some believe that as people get older, the typically physical ways of sharing love become less important than the actual meaning and emotions that accompany these feelings. Yet there are others, particularly in this day and age of Viagra, who are thrilled to have the opportunity to continue experiencing love's lust, and to them, that becomes the priority.

From a cultural perspective, the message seems to be very clear: love is only for the young and beautiful, that people over 65 are no longer interested in or suited for things such as romance and passion. I don't know about you, but I don't believe this for a second and I've seen enough proof to prove it. What really troubles me though, is that there are many older adults who actually believe and agree with this outdated cultural perspective. And if one closes out possibilities before even having the chance to experience them, then that's missing out on life.

There are a number of ways people can experience love in their lives. I've known widows and widowers, who meet at a retirement community, date, fall in love, and often get married. And as sweet as it may sound, there's often a disgruntled family member in the background who thinks it's ridiculous and causes an unnecessary and uncomfortable mess. There are other stories of those who've lost a spouse and unknowingly, suddenly find themselves back in the dating scene -- a very unfamiliar place they likely haven't seen in many, many years that leaves them full of anxiety and apprehension on just what to do next. And then there are others who channel their emotions of love into projects, pets and/or people that also provide true meaning in their lives.

Whichever route we choose, what matters most is companionship, and what we feel in our heart. At no age or stage in our life does this really change. What does change however, is the method we utilize to maintain this in our lives. Whether you choose to volunteer, rescue a pet, reach out to someone in need, or go the traditional route of seeking a partner, the true essence of love is giving of ourselves to someone or something else. Create the opportunity to make a positive difference in someone's life through a simple smile or friendly deed and you too will experience the real meaning of love.

Making A Difference
&

Retirement means different things to different people. Some choose to take it easy and relax away the days, while others are so involved they wonder how they ever had time for work. But regardless of the path you select, there are definitely certain aspects that contribute to one's overall satisfaction during this phase of life -- and it's beyond just personal pleasure.

Since today's average American spends about one-third of their life in retirement, and in relatively good health, the options are plentiful -- from travel to recreation, to work and volunteering, to just being. But more and more studies are reporting the connection between life satisfaction and engagement -- and I'm not referring to the matrimonial type. It's about staying connected, having a sense of meaning and purpose to your activities.

Life satisfaction, at any age, basically revolves around three main components: body, mind, and spirit. We need to focus our energy on taking care of ourselves physically, keeping ourselves mentally sharp, and participating in activities that fulfill our spirit. The latter is often one that is overlooked, yet those who choose to give of themselves and make a difference in someone else's life, make a profoundly positive difference in their own life as well.

There are numerous worthy causes to be involved in but I've always been particularly fond of the intergenerational programs that link seniors with children -- especially those helping with learning. The lifelong impact these one-on-one relationships can have is extraordinary, and by evidence of the continual growing need for volunteers, the schools really do win, too!

A national program offered through OASIS offers seniors the opportunity to serve as reading tutors. The OASIS program that has grown exponentially with over 350,000 participants since its inception in 1983.

"No special skills or background are required other than a caring attitude and a willingness to help, " said one of the program coordinators. "We provide the training, which ranges from a brief overview for classroom tutors to two hours for a Grandfriend Mentor, and twelve hours to become a one-on-one OASIS tutor.

"This is such a win-win for everyone involved," the coordinator said. "The children benefit from the extra attention they receive from these seniors, the teachers and schools benefit from the extra pairs of helping hands, and the seniors gain a sense of satisfaction and joy seeing what a difference they make. "

The reasons and benefits seniors get involved are as varied as the people themselves. Gordon Record, 68, always wanted to be a teacher but his career took him in a different direction. But after retiring from the DPW after thirty-two years, he knew he wanted to do something with kids in the community as a way of giving back.

"I hoped I'd be able to make a difference, and after seeing the effect this program has had on the kids -- and the parents, too, it has been tremendously satisfying," Gordon said.

Apparently so, because Gordon has expanded his involvement from being a tutor to now include being a Grandfriend too, which he says is an equally rewarding mentoring role.

For septuagenarian Ellen Cooksy, she takes her love of art into the third grade classroom every Tuesday and has even recruited some of her fellow friends from the local Art Association to join her.

"The enthusiasm and excitement of the kids literally lights up my life," Ellen said. "And I don't just teach arts and crafts, this is real art -- from basic drawing to color, shapes, and I even have a docent from the local Museum of Art come and give an educational talk with slides and then we follow that up with a field trip to the Museum the following week."

Ellen believes art should be a part of every child's education, but with all the budget cuts, few schools are able to provide it anymore. Additionally, Ellen admits that she misses being around children. Although she has twelve grandchildren, she doesn't see them enough, so this helps fill that void too.

"These kids are so terrific and very, very appreciative of all we do," Ellen said. "They give us hugs, smiles, and lots of thank-you's, -- and if that isn't reward enough, I don't know what is. It makes you feel so good inside to know you're making a difference in someone else's life -- especially a child's, because that can last a lifetime."

So instead of just planning your next tee time or holiday cruise, consider the life satisfaction experienced by people like Ellen, whose next dream is to take her art program to the children on one of the Indian reservations.

National Aging Conference Report

&

More than four thousand professionals in aging converged upon the city by the bay in San Francisco for the annual Joint Conference of the American Society on Aging and the National Council on Aging, where the top experts from around the country presented the latest thinking and research on a myriad of subjects.

Attendees pursued over one thousand sessions in more than fifty different topic areas including family care giving, retirement, Medicare/Social Security reform, grand parenting, lifelong learning, the aging workforce, health promotion and wellness, innovations in long term care, business concerns, and even sexuality in the longevity revolution.

With the theme of this year's conference, "The Road Ahead: Taking the Journey Together," it was enlightening to see the focus addressing not only current issues, but perhaps more importantly, innovative discussions on the upcoming challenges and opportunities of an aging society, particularly as the Baby Boomer generation starts turning 50 (which is happening at a rate of one every seven seconds), and by 2011, the first of this largest generation in history will begin turning 65.

The Baby Boomers have always had a powerful influence on society, primarily due to their numbers. Between 1946 and 1964, 76 million people were born, one-third of our total population. And just as they've had a major impact on every phase of life they've experienced, their effect on aging is expected to be no different.

One thing baby boomers are definitely good at is raising awareness. In many ways, they created the childcare issues because with so many women working, their numbers enabled them to demand social change and the development of programs to assist them in juggling their work and home responsibilities. They are also likely to generate a similar form of assistance with their upcoming eldercare needs, especially since it's estimated that the average family can expect to spend more time caring for an aging parent than their own children. And it's projected that today's boomers will likely have more parents to care for than they have children. Look for more national programs, services and providers to help here and/or perhaps a tax break as a more immediate response to assist with this issue.

The concept of retirement is also likely to change. Of course, taking lead from today's active and healthy retirees who are so involved they often wonder how they ever had time to work, in many ways it already has. The idea of fishing and golfing is being replaced by a desire to continue being productive and experiencing new options. Of course, many are taking time to enjoy some leisure time as well, just not exclusively.

Perhaps of utmost concern is the economics of retirement and increased longevity. Coupled with the reality of a growing debt ratio and decreased savings, financial gerontology was a new subject at this year's conference, as there is growing concern many people will likely outlive their money. With people spending one third of their life in retirement -- an estimated thirty years, coupled with the Social Security Administration's estimate that only 8 of every 100 people will have adequate income after working forty years, changes are definitely going to have to be made.

Optimal Aging

&

F ew will deny the fact that the health and fitness industry as a whole, has failed in getting more Americans to
exercise. There are as many theories as to why this is
as there are excuses not to exercise. Yet much of the blame
has consistently centered on the industry's emphasis on mere
physical appearances (what we look like) versus the real
health benefits that occur physiologically on the inside.

The good news is this is finally beginning to change.
Forget the 'Aeroba-Bunny' exercise concept. The reality today
is that there are significant health benefits to exercise -- and
it's clearly evident we're never too old to do so. In fact, we're
too old not to!

IDEA Health & Fitness Association, the world's leading membership organization of health and fitness professionals, with more than 19K members in more than 80 countries,
has also recognized a better way to motivate more to get
active. At their national convention, the evening's most covet-
ed award for "Inspirational Athlete of the Year," was presented
to Bert Morrow, a 92-year old world record hurdler who earlier in the day competed in the local Senior Olympics and won
three gold medals in the 80m Hurdles, the 100m Sprint and
the 200m Sprint.

While running the hurdles as an octogenarian is
impressive enough, the fact that Bert had a pacemaker put in
five days after his 89th birthday, makes his story all the more

extraordinary. When he walked into the hospital with a pulse rate of 30, the doctors were amazed he hadn't suffered a heart attack or stroke and credited his healthy lifestyle as the reason.

But Bert seems to be one who defies the odds. Proving it's never too late, Bert didn't even run his first hurdle until the age of 69 and claims he was a physical wreck in his 40's and 50's. Today he'll tell you he's healthier than ever and his recent pacemaker check-up proves it.

"The technology has evolved so much that we really can improve the quality of life for people," said a representative for Guidant pacemaker. "Bert's doing great. His own heart has been beating 99% of the time, so the pacemaker's there strictly as a back-up, which gives Bert the peace of mind to keep on doing what he loves to do -- hurdling!"

The technology is incredible. In Bert's follow-up cardiology appointment, the doctor hooked his pacemaker up to a computer and was able to get an accurate daily reading of Bert's heart rate for the previous eight months.

"What were you doing on June 29 at 10:00 a.m. Bert?" Savage asked. "I was in the starting blocks for the 80m Hurdle race!" Bert answered. "Well that explains the big change in heart rate I see," Savage said. "And what about May 26 and May 11, what happened then?" Bert thought for a minute and remembered, "I was competing in Long Beach and Irvine on those dates, too!"

Bert was absolutely amazed at the detail of this test, and equally thrilled that the results confirmed what he had been feeling.

"I've felt great ever since the surgery. And to know all's well with my ticker too, makes me want to tell everyone about the importance of eating right and getting regular exercise," Bert said. "I'd probably be dead otherwise!"

Although Bert is recognized for his unbelievable hurdling abilities, it's usually his physical appearance that generates a lot of the attention. But the real story is how he's been able to achieve these remarkable feats -- what he's done on the inside is what made the real difference.

The world needs more role models like Bert Morrow. Not to go out and run hurdles necessarily, but to understand the connection between healthy lifestyle choices and vital aging.

It's no coincidence that Bert was a physical wreck in his earlier years due to his hectic, inactive lifestyle. Since turning that around, he's become an impressive specimen of optimal aging, void of the typical age-related health problems seen in people his age -- or even half his age, frankly.

He's certainly not invincible, the pacemaker proves that. But it does demonstrate Bert's belief to never give up. Although he had to cut back on his activities during his healing, he never wavered from his goal to hurdle again, and it's likely that goal contributed greatly to his recovery.

Bert is an example of optimal aging, and that's why he received this award. By looking at his life from the inside out, rather than just the outside in, we can better understand how what we think and do on the inside does affect both who we are and what we become on the outside.

Beliefs play a powerful role in our lives, particularly regarding the choices we make. So if mindset, attitudes and beliefs drive behaviors, that's something we must always remember in our effort to live healthy, happy, long lives.

The Psycho-Spiritual Dimensions of Aging
&

I recently attended a lecture at The Sam and Rose Stein Institute for Research on Aging at the University of California at San Diego (UCSD), recognized as one of the top sites in the country for age related studies, titled "Staying Young: The Psycho-Spiritual Dimensions of Aging," conducted by staff member, J. Adam Milgram, M.A.

With an advanced degree in psychology, 25 years experience in this field, and serving as a family counselor and educator, Milgram said he recently added this "spiritual component" to his work in psychology in an effort to awaken people to life and all of its potential.

As evidence by the turnout, apparently a number of people are curious about this dimension of life and intrigued by the non-tangible "spiritual" aspect of aging. The reference to "spiritual" was not religious in its intent, but rather in essence, revolves around the aspect of being -- how to live in the here and now and have it be a positive experience. It is more a question of determining what kind of life you want to have while you're living, and how does one create meaning in their life.

From the beginning, Milgram admitted he did not have all the answers, but rather this was a session to share thoughts toward a better understanding of life, as well as aging. The fact that much of today's aging research indicates the role and responsibility individuals play in determining how long and how well we live (current studies state that 70% of the characteristics of aging are based on lifestyle, while only 30% are based on genetics), is both empowering and frightening. But at the same time, life, no matter what age you are, can also be looked at as a challenge or opportunity. Like lifestyle, much of it does revolve around the choices we make.

With regard to aging, most people generally categorize this phase of life as more of a challenge than an opportunity. But as Milgram indicated, opportunities appear when we take on these challenges. Life provides the opportunity to create ourselves at all stages -- we are what we make ourselves to be.

"In our society, even though there are doors that open and doors that close, we generally focus more on the doors that close," Milgram said. "We often have a pessimistic view of aging and tend to focus more on the negative changes. Yes, there are changes and we must face these challenges. But from challenge comes the opportunity to face new experiences, extend our consciousness of who we are beyond our mere physical being and tune-in within to other matters of the heart, and soul, etc."

Perhaps one of the most important aspects of aging, and often one of the least discussed, is the understanding of having a sense of meaning and purpose in our life and the value of staying involved in meaningful activities. One of my favorite centenarians described it to me as the difference between living and existing. Granted there are limitations in every phase of life, but if we let them dictate us toward disengagement or withdrawal from life, that's when it can be detrimental.

Milgram described this as "conscious aging," where you're aware of the changes that are occurring as you age, and consciously decide how you'll deal with them.

"There's nothing new about self-responsibility," he said. "We are responsible for our own well-being. It's not our doctors job, it's our job."

We all must be consciously aware of the role we play in both the aging process, and in life itself. If we don't have challenges as we grow older and challenge ourselves with new activities and innovative ways to deal with life's changes, then we're just walking around like zombies missing opportunities. We've got to go at it everyday and not focus exclusively on what we don't have and instead, do the best with what we do have!

Redefining Retirement: Life Option Centers

&

I've long believed that one of the most significant challenges we face with aging in this country is the mere word "retirement." Its definition and image signifies disengaging -- yet study after study on "successful aging" indicates that in actuality, engagement -- staying involved with challenging, meaningful, and purposeful activities is the healthiest and most satisfying way to grow older.

This, of course, is where the dichotomy comes in. On the one hand, we've been a society that believes one should rest and relax in their later years -- but at the same time, studies of those who've been there clearly shows that the healthiest and most satisfying option is just the opposite of what the word "retirement" implies.

Changing the way people think and view retirement could be one of the most exciting things we'll see in the field of aging. There's a huge opportunity to better service the transition for people from work to other life options -- to help retirees discover what they want to do with the second half of their lives."

For as long as I can remember, the field of aging has predominantly focused on addressing the problem issues. But aging isn't all about just problems and aren't we really missing the boat if we don't look at the opportunities as well?

A new concept for senior centers is emerging -- Life Option Centers would provide a place for direction and connection to the array of possibilities available in the second half of life. Think of it as something similar to the college campus' Student Union -- a hangout to discover what you might want to do during the next phase of your life. A place where you can go to socialize, or get direction on where you can take classes, visit with a retirement counselor, or even connect with job opportunities, transportation and/or housing options, travel possibilities, community resources or even finding meaningful volunteer ideas.

A Life Options Center is being described as a "transition central," a hub for direction and connection to help people decide how to make the most of their midlife and later years.

As an AARP retirement specialist, it's always surprising to me how so many people spend more time planning a two-week vacation than the one-third of their life they'll spend in retirement. But perhaps this is due to the negative image people have of aging and retirement -- it's not known as a healthy, fulfilling stage of life so people apparently just avoid thinking of the negative and therefore do virtually little planning, if any.

The reality, however, is that the majority of us will be healthy and vital for most of this time. But financial planning seems to be the only planning that's done, if any -- leaving little thought to what we'll do with this new time we'll have. It's kind of ironic in a sense, that all our working adult life we never seem to have enough time -- yet in retirement, we have an abundance of it and don't know what to do with it.

Retirement is not just about a time without responsibility and obligation, yet this lack of structure has a tendency to make some believe it's just an eternal holiday. But after a few fishing trips, cruises, and/or outings on the links, people get bored and discover a need for something else in their life -- but what?

This is where the biggest secret may be -- the importance of having meaning in your life. Keeping the body healthy and the mind stimulated are two of the three components of successful aging and retirement, but continuing to have/find meaning in your life is equally essential. I actually believe this final factor could be the most important element of all.

With 20-30 years of life available to us in retirement -- that's a lot of time to contribute to something meaningful. It doesn't necessarily mean that it has to be work, but the word "work" does take on an entirely different connotation when you're participating in an activity you enjoy, that stimulates and challenges you while also making a positive difference in someone else's life or the world itself.

Maybe you could become a master at something you've never done before, or teach/mentor people about something you're passionate about and know well. Or maybe you could devote your energies to several needy community programs, or explore areas of the world that fascinate you. Maybe you want to work and/or volunteer but aren't sure in what capacity -- or travel with an education program but don't know how to connect with it.

It's time to re-invent retirement. It's not about a second childhood, but rather a new phase of life with meaning to do some of our best work -- an opportunity to add not only years to our life, but life to our years.

Perhaps retirement will soon be looked at as an interim period to be done in phases -- where we take a break between periods of doing, contributing, volunteering, working, and/or traveling, catch our breath and then make our next transition to another phase/chapter of life that embodies a whole new definition of success with a distinctive combination of learning, growth, and contribution.

A new story of what is possible and desirable in later life and retirement is needed -- and we just may be on our way to achieving it.

Rest Equals Rust

%

There appears to be quite a lot of interest in healthy aging these days. And with more and more "super seniors" out there living by example, we're learning some interesting new things.

Bert Morrow, 91, is a world record hurdler who didn't even run his first hurdle till the age of 69. He claims he was a physical wreck in his 40s and 50s, and says he's healthier now than he ever was then, after making some significant lifestyle changes.

Morrow credits the importance of stretching and the benefits of eating a healthy diet as being key to his success. His breakfast cereal recipe consists of 14 different grains he soaks overnight, drains and then eats like cereal with milk, sliced banana on top, and then what he calls his energy producing secret weapon: bee pollen.

"Scientists have identified 22 antioxidants in bee pollen and two additional ones they believe may be responsible for its energy-generating component," Morrow stated. "It's certainly worked for me -- I've been using it for years. I can have my breakfast early in the morning, drive up to Los Angeles for a track meet, run all day in my different events while just drinking water throughout the day, and still have enough energy to drive home and have dinner!"

Morrow has become a celebrity of sorts, due to having broken five world records in the hurdles, including breaking his own record twice. And today he's still at it -- chasing the world record to become the oldest hurdler in the world.

Two other favorite super senior friends of mine are June and Harvey Tatro, 91 and 95, who just celebrated their 69th wedding anniversary. They believe whole-heartedly that both exercise and a positive attitude are the keys to their success.

June, in many ways, is a national treasure as she has been teaching older adult fitness classes for over 40 years. Although Harvey has had a variety of health problems, he says he's been able to overcome and recuperate from all of them due to his positive perspective and participation in his wife's classes.

"I've had every health problem there is -- but I'm still here, I feel great, and I know my wife's classes have helped me get healthy quickly again even after heart surgery," Harvey claimed. "And I'll tell you another thing, worrying never did anybody a bit of good, so instead of being down about things, turn that energy into positive thoughts and you'll be a lot better off. Our thoughts project our body's physical response so it's extremely important to stay positive for good health, otherwise that negative thinking will just generate into some other health problem."

The research confirms what the Tatros believe. Karl Knopf, Ph.D., and one of the pioneers in the field of adult fitness, has been teaching functional fitness and strength training to seniors long before it was fashionable. His philosophy is, "when you rest, you rust," so he teaches people about the benefits of staying active throughout life.

"Rest is actually one of the worst things for older adults because research studies today indicate that it's the physical inactivity that is most hazardous to our health," Knopf stated.

Knopf addresses a variety of issues including the powerful role of self-responsibility and choices in determining the status of our later years. And considering the fact that prevention is cheaper and less toxic than prescriptions, more and more older adults seem to be interested in taking this proactive stance.

"What you do today will determine how you age tomorrow," Knopf stated. "So just doing a little bit today will help you be a little better tomorrow, and the accumulation of these healthy habits will add up in your favor down the road."

Knopf explains that being active and healthy throughout life (although he also states that it's never too late to start healthy habits) ultimately can result in compressing the amount of time people spend in frailty or poor health.

"Most people live too short and die too long as wrote Walter Bortz, M.D. and author of the book with the same title," Knopf shared. "By age 70, for example, most people have lost 50% of their strength due to lack of use and decon-ditioning -- which makes it very difficult for people to then continue performing the activities of daily living. Research now shows that this loss can actually be reversed through proper resistance exercises. So it's not just age necessarily, that creates the decline -- and that's good news because we can therefore do something to prevent and/or reverse that sup-posed inevitable loss."

Knopf states an amazing example to make his point. Those who are active age at a rate of only 1/2% per year ver-sus those who aren't active age at a rate of 2% per year. Over the course of 20 years that can make a significant difference: the active group aged just 10% while the non-active group aged 40% over the same course of time.

"The difference is marked in one's quality of life and that's the measure that really counts," Knopf said. "When a person is operating optimally physically, mentally, socially, and culturally, that's successful aging -- being able to enjoy life and continue doing the things you like!"

SUPERSENIOR CELEBS

&

Dodo Cheney, 87

&

Women's Tennis Pioneer, Champion and Legend

A true pioneer of women's tennis, Dorothy "Dodo" Cheney, has competed in competitive tennis for eight decades -- from her teens to super senior years.

As the first American woman to win the Australian National Championships in 1938, Cheney has won 343 USTA National Titles, 20 Senior Grand Slams and was recently inducted into the International Tennis Hall of Fame alongside tennis greats, Steffi Graf and Stefan Edberg.

While many tennis aficionados felt Cheney's Hall of Fame induction was long overdue, Cheney was thrilled with the honor, regardless of when it happened.

"This was the best year to have been inducted because it was the 50th Anniversary, so all the previous inductees were there too," Cheney shared. "There was a big gala with dinner and dancing -- which I did lots of with my family and even with my arthritic knees. I didn't feel any pain so I guess I'll just have to keep on dancing too!"

It's likely Cheney's feet haven't touched the ground since getting the call about her induction. When asked who she wanted to introduce her at the prestigious ceremony, Cheney didn't hesitate and said, "Johnny McEnroe."

A big fan of Cheney's McEnroe may deserve partial credit for Cheney's induction since he referred to her as being overlooked by the Hall during his induction speech, so he happily accepted the honor and Cheney's request to introduce her at this year's ceremony.

"What a thrill it was for an 87-year old grandma, well actually, great-great grandma, to be escorted around center court by Johnny Mac!" Cheney cheered.

But McEnroe didn't stop there; he later invited Cheney to hit with him on one of the outer courts, to which Cheney thought he had to be joking.

"After the ceremony, Johnny asked if I wanted to go hit and I thought certainly he was kidding, but he wasn't," Cheney remembered. "We got our rackets and off we went. We had a ball! Of course, he made me look good -- hit 'em right to me and I even scooted a few up the line right by him, but I'm sure he missed them on purpose!" Cheney laughed.

According to Cheney, McEnroe told her she was the only woman player to take him up on his offer, saying Venus Williams and other top players had always declined.

But Cheney's always up for a challenge and some fun so she has no intention of stopping playing the game she loves. With more titles than anyone in the sport, or "gold balls," as Cheney refers to them, the word retirement is virtually non-existent in her vocabulary. She has actually won titles in singles, doubles and mixed doubles for every age group category she has ever played in and still continues to rack up the trophies in the U.S. Women's 85+ division today.

Cheney's obviously still in great shape, still loves the game and maintains her competitive drive, so it should be no surprise she continues to thrive.

"I think our 85+ age group is doing a good job teaching people the benefits of tennis for life," Cheney said. "At the Hall of Fame induction, you should have seen all of us older players -- we're still healthy and looking pretty good, and that's what tennis does."

Cheney credits her family support and her genes (her parents were both pro tennis champions) as key to her longevity. She and her daughter still compete and win Mother-Daughter championships, and Cheney says her son-in-law doctor helps keep her healthy too.

"I love tennis and am so thankful I can still play this game. I owe so much to tennis and just hope I can give something back, so others will love it too!" Cheney exclaimed.

Spoken like a true champion and a definite legend.

Walter Cronkite

&

Wisdom

W alter Cronkite, 85, is a member of what has been called the "Greatest Generation," and is one of the most recognized television news anchors in broadcast history.

In an address to a standing-room only crowd at an AARP national convention, Cronkite mesmerized the audience with entertaining tales from the past and insightful responses to today's issues.

After spending 20 years at the CBS evening-news network desk, starting in 1962, Cronkite has certainly seen his share of changes.

"I saw the world change -- from historic events to hairstyles, including my own!" he laughed. "But the '60s were undoubtedly tumultuous, the most amazing," Cronkite continued. "My teary-eyed account of the J.F.Kennedy assassination was one of the most difficult, and the landing on the moon presented an emotional challenge of a different kind. I had as long as NASA to prepare what I'd say, but somehow, when that vehicle actually landed on the moon, I was literally speechless. It was such a difficult time in our country then, but this was a great piece of positive news, so uplifting and hopeful."

Seeing Cronkite live, on stage, felt just like he was sitting in our living room, minus the TV box that usually surrounded him. His blue eyes still sparkle and his warm, friendly personality became ever apparent when he asked the technical crew to turn up the house lights so he could "see the folks."

Cronkite then preceded to answer questions from the audience, which ranged from what was his most memorable news experience to his biggest regret, as well as his opinion of today's media and the state of the war dilemma in Iraq.

"There was nothing like covering a war for memorable experiences," Cronkite said. "I was certainly one of the most active war correspondents, having flown in B52 Bombers during Vietnam, landing at Normandy in WWII and covering the Battle of the Bulge was amazing, under the leadership of General Patton."

As far as the current state of today's media and the interest to raise the bar as far as quality goes, Cronkite quickly explained that the industry has changed drastically.

"Too much time is spent on trivial news -- celebrities and scandals," Cronkite said, to which the audience responded with thunderous applause. "But it's not because we don't have good journalists, it's a reflection of how the industry has changed. All these cable channels have created stiff competition for the advertising dollar. It's not like it used to be when the three major networks each controlled upwards of 30% of the television audience for the evening news. Today the percentage is half that, if they're lucky, and therefore management's priorities are ratings, unfortunately. Instead of trying to improve the product, they generally have to cut production costs to save money. There are just too many fingers in the pie and that's what's really affecting the quality. Competition is fierce."

     Although Cronkite claims he still misses his work and being in the newsroom, he has no regrets. "I'm quite satisfied with my life. I'm happy with my wife and family, and being here with all of you," he said. "I don't find it useful to sit around thinking of lost opportunities. Sure, there might be some aspect of a story I might regret not pursuing, but I still write and work on documentaries. But I'd also like to be back in the newsroom helping set the agenda and maybe I will again, someday."

With regard to the current dilemma in Iraq and the United Nations, Cronkite strongly believes the best agenda for the U.S. is to have both the support of its people and the U.N. But he also couldn't help to wonder if war is always the best answer.

"We spend billions of dollars determining how to kill the most people with destructive weapons, but shouldn't we also consider spending a similar amount of money on how to achieve peace?" Cronkite asked. "Settling differences with death is not the only answer."

Such words of wisdom generally only come with time and experience and it's plain to see that the great Walter Cronkite still has them both.

Phyllis Diller, 87

&

Lady of Laughter

T hey say laughter is the best medicine, and there are few on the planet who have given us more laughs than Phyllis Diller. The 'Lady of Laughter' and I met at the debut of the world premiere of her documentary, "Goodnight, We Love You," and although not yet in full distribution, it's a hit and a definite must see for people of all ages.

After 47 years in show biz, Phyllis Diller performed her final show on May 5, 2002, in Las Vegas, to a sold out crowd of fans, family and friends. The film includes clips from the show, while also capturing a never-before-seen look at Diller, who opened her heart and home by providing unprecedented access to her preparations for her final performance and insight to her life behind the scenes.

Diller, the comic legend who looks fabulous and appears to still have what it takes to continue performing, when asked why it was time to stop said, "I'm too old. By the time you get really great, you're too old to do it!" she said, followed by her classic trademark, "Ha!" -- which is not a stage act, it's her genuine laugh -- the real deal.

Although she claims age as one of the reasons for stopping (Diller quotes her age as "three years short of 90"), in the same breath and with that same style that has endeared so many, she quickly made jokes of this stage of life -- just as

she has with most other aspects of her life, that has won her many fans since the beginning.

"You know you're old when your walker has an airbag, your birth certificate is a scroll, and your blood type has been discontinued!"

Yet all kidding aside, Diller said of her stage performing, "Honestly, it just came time to say good-bye. I've watched some of my colleagues stay too long, but I'd rather stop at the top."

Frankly, it's hard to imagine Phyllis Diller ever not at the top, regardless of when she stops. Of course, the reality is that she's really not stopping -- she's just getting off the road.

"It's the grind of travel more than anything," Diller said. "I used to love to fly. But as a grandmother and being undressed by airport security, it's just not for me anymore."

While some thought her final show would be a difficult task for someone who has been in this business for almost half a century, Diller claims it really wasn't hard because she has so many other interests and things she wants to do. She's particularly excited about pursuing her second career, painting. Without any formal instruction, Diller is an impressionist painter who has sold over 500 pieces of her work since starting in her 60s.

Diller has always been somewhat of a late bloomer, and one who rarely did things in the traditional way. She truly was a pioneer, America's first stand-up female comic in history. And she didn't even break into the once male dominated industry until 1955, at almost age 40, when she was both a wife and mother of five.

"Since I was older, I had a lot of good material to work
with," Diller said. "I was different. Being the first female, I
talked about things that hadn't been discussed before. It was a
rough crowd back then. Smoke-filled rooms, drinking, mostly
men - and out I walk on stage. But they could relate to me.
I'd talk about being a wife - not putting men down, but instead
making fun of myself."

Keeping a sense of humor about life is certainly one of
the secrets to living a healthy, happy, long life -- and likely
one of the reasons Diller is so comfortable in her own skin.
Of course, she's had some adjustments to that as well, but like
most other things, she's found lots of humor (as we all have),
in that too.

"There are no two parts of my body the same age!"
Diller said. "I've had so much fixed, when I die, God won't
recognize me!" she laughed. "I personally, brought cosmetic
surgery out of the closet."

It's true. In fact, Diller is often referred to as the
'Queen of Cosmetic Surgery,' and the Academy of Cosmetic
Surgery even honored her for generating awareness for their
industry. The reality is, she looks great. And more importantly, she feels great too. She recognizes people have always
been fascinated by all she's had done and actually remembers
when she used to provide reporters with a typed list of all her
procedures since it was always asked of her in interviews and
sometimes she couldn't remember them all. She was always
honest, and this way, consistent too.

But Diller will be the first to tell you that it wasn't
about being younger, but more importantly, being the best she
could be and looking good. Actually, she thinks much of her
popularity was due to her looks -- not that she was so striking-
ly beautiful, but rather that she was always so different looking.

"I started the Punk look," Diller said. "My hairdo was chic and my wild, bed-head look is still hip today!"

For any talent to achieve 47 years of success, particularly in an industry that worships youth and glamour, Diller always kept things fresh by regularly changing her look. And she had an array of options to select from. In fact, on the road she was known to travel with some 60 suitcases filled with all her gear. At home, she has entire rooms for all her clothes, glasses, wigs, bags, shoes and hats. She even invented clear hatboxes so she could see which hat was where. It was all part of the act - you never knew what she'd look like next and that was part of what kept her fresh and endeared by so many.

Diller always beat to her own drum and claims it's a philosophy she's maintained since her beginning. "I just do what I do, sometimes without even testing the water," Diller said. "I don't let fear or criticism stop me. Never did, and I never will."

This philosophy is particularly obvious when you look at some of her interests. Probably one of her most notable is her love and fascination with cars -- not typical of most women, and definitely not during the early days. Yet still today, Diller talks admirably about her Excalibur (an Excalibur 1927 Mercedes Phaeton) that is so impressive it's soon going to be in the Peterson Auto Museum in Los Angeles.

"I'm so proud that a lot of other people will now get to adore that car as much as I did, and still do," Diller said. "The horn plays the theme from the film 'The Bridge on The River Kwai' and I also customized it with power steering because otherwise, not even Arnold Schwarzenegger could park it!

Diller, who always dressed for the part, even did so when she took this car out for a spin. Complete with big goggle glasses, hat and scarf -- she was a definite site to be seen! And likely, hard to miss.

Yet never one to miss an opportunity for laughs, Diller always found humor in her driving as well. "I'm a lousy driver. I never know if it's 1:00 PM or if I'm going 100! I have a phone in the car now too -- I hit a phone booth!" she laughed.

One of Diller's other surprise attributes is her musical inclination. She's actually a trained musician who studied piano all her life and even performed Bach and Beethoven with more than 100 symphony orchestras. She'd initially appear on stage with funny hats and perform a few comedy bits from the piano, and then she'd play the keyboard with such amazing talent it often astounded audiences. But most of all, Diller loved it. Playing with the symphonies was like a dream come true to her.

In a more traditional sense, Diller says the kitchen is her favorite room because she loves to cook. In fact, there were many times when she claims she carried a kitchen with her on the road.

"I liked to unwind by cooking after the show," Diller said. "It was part of my therapy. Plus, it's your life, and I wanted to eat healthy so I brought my own stuff with me."

Health-wise today, Diller calls herself the "Bionic Woman," considering she has a pacemaker for congestive heart failure after suffering a major heart attack years ago. Not expected to live, Diller stopped breathing three different times during the episode and as a result of surviving, she appreciates each new day that much more now -- and lives each one to the fullest.

But of all the things she appreciates most, it's her fans and family that top the list. She always personally signed all the autographs for her fans (unlike many other celebrities whose signings are often phony) and she regularly performs at numerous charitable events, in an effort to give back as much as possible.

While her fans and the industry have awarded her with countless accolades, honors and tributes, Diller, while grateful, says she is still proudest of her children, their accomplishments and contributions and the good times they continue to share as a family.

Diller is indeed an icon and one whose legacy will undoubtedly live on. There's only one Phyllis Diller, and as she closes this chapter in her book of life, may we be privileged enough to experience more of her upcoming chapters in this new phase of life.

Goodnight, Phyllis … we love you too.

Diane Keaton, 58

&

Something's Gotta Give

It's obvious the rules of aging are changing. When block-buster movies start featuring "older" actors with a combined age of 125, who fall in love with these later-in-life romances where the old guy actually wins the heart of the actress over the younger, sexier stud -- that's a sign there's something new going on here.

In the blockbuster movie, "Something's Gotta Give," starring Diane Keaton, 58, who won the Golden Globe award for Best Actress and also received an Academy Award nomination for her work with co-star Jack Nicholson, 67, it's ironic that initially, the studios and investors had to be convinced a movie about a 50+ year old woman finding love would sell. But it did - and it sold big, too!

This movie hit so many real life targets that it should be required viewing for everyone 50+. In fact, it wouldn't be a bad flick for everyone at any age to see in order to better understand the dynamics involved with living longer, healthier lives and the effect this will continue to have on relationships, families, etc.

Particularly poignant to me were the rave reviews critics gave Keaton, in a strange, complimentary way, for how great she looked "for a woman her age!"

What? Are you kidding me? She looked fabulous for a woman of ANY age, let alone, 50-something, appearing naked for the first time in a career that spans more than forty films -- many considered classics, with already one Academy Award and two other Oscar nominations.

This mode of thinking has got to change if you ask me. And particularly in the youth-obsessed Hollywood world that is so powerful in establishing trends -- or documenting them. By sheer evidence of this movie's success, it's obvious there's a huge market out there waiting for this type of story line. And if the studios and powers-to-be are smart, they'll make a note of this and continue to move more positively forward.

I don't' know if this movie was made before or after the recent success of "Calendar Girls" but it's perfectly clear to me that this new image of aging phenomenon is the real deal and the sooner and more frequently these types of films are brought mainstream, the better off this planet will be.

But maybe we're already heading in that direction. Interestingly enough, it was the young, sensitive, doctor love interest played by Keanu Reeves, who was so enamored with Keaton's character. Even though there was a 20-year age difference (with Keaton being the older woman), it was Reeves' character who said, "age is just a number and it has nothing to do with falling in love."

The wealthy cad played by Nicholson, who had never dated a woman older than 30, finally realized what was really important in life after experiencing a life-changing wake-up call. He fell in love with Keaton, and won her heart -- a heart she herself, had given up on ever finding love again. So while love interests certainly don't have to reflect a significant age difference, in some cases, it's perfectly OK if they do.

"Something's Gotta Give" is a classic -- and definitely evident that something's starting to change.

Jack LaLanne, 90

&

"You Gotta Believe to Achieve!"

T here's a lot of interest in the concept of vitality -- what it is, how you can get it, and why it's so essential to living a healthy, happy life. As keynote speakers at a Vital Aging conference, Jack and Elaine LaLanne addressed this topic and shared their insight as to how we can all attain it. Believe it or not, it's all about beliefs.

First and foremost, Jack and Elaine clarified that vitality is not just one thing -- it involves many things: keeping yourself challenged mentally and physically, staying engaged in life by participating in various activities, maintaining a spiritual aspect, volunteering and doing for others. Of course, practicing good health habits with a healthy diet and regular exercise is also essential because that's the battery that keeps us all going.

Most everyone seems to identify Jack LaLanne with exercise, but those who really know him know that his message of healthy eating and diet is equally important. One of his favorite quotes is, "If man made it, don't eat it and if it tastes good, spit it out!" And he practices what he preaches, he never eats between meals and hasn't had a bite of white sugar in over 70 years!

Yet what really makes Jack tick is his effort in encouraging people to recognize that the most important person in the world is you! You have to take care of you. No one else is going to do it, but we each have to want to do it, too -- and believe we can.

Perhaps that's the real issue. It seems there are a lot of people, regardless of age, who just aren't real excited about life or their role in it. So maybe that's the first step: to find our passion -- to have passion for life, enthusiasm for life, by staying involved, staying connected, having a sense of meaning and purpose in your life, and feeling like there's a reason for living and an opportunity to continue contributing. That's really living -- anything less is merely existing.

"If you don't care about the most important person in your life -- you, then you must be psycho!" Jack claims. But of course, Jack will also tell you that he's certainly been considered a psycho himself -- but that was only what others thought, never what Jack believed.

Back in 1931, when Jack first got involved in the fitness field, most everyone thought he was psycho. People thought he was literally nuts -- one sandwich short of a picnic -- talking about the benefits of strength training and exercise for a healthy life. But Jack didn't care what others thought because he knew the truth. He lived it, experienced it, and saw the results in himself and others he trained, so he knew that if he just stuck to it, he would ultimately lead by example.

Well, there's no doubt that he's done that. But what many may not know is that this is Jack's life mission, his life's work, his passion, and that is what has created his vitality. Some call it a "joie de vive," (love of life) or reason for living. Regardless of what you call it, everyone has to have a reason for being and when and if you're lucky enough to find your life's work, then you too, will have the desire and motivation to take care of yourself so that you can continue living and doing what you love to do. Ultimately, it's all about doing something that makes a positive difference.

There are undoubtedly many people on this planet who've never found their life's work, and in many ways, have lived a life that has perhaps felt unfulfilling. Well, like vitality, you can't just find your life's work and passion in a pill, bottle, or book. You've got to experience life by trying lots of different things to find what makes you tick -- feel alive and emotionally charged up. This takes work, and frankly, it's hard work. But as the saying goes, anything worthwhile in life takes effort. You get out what you put in, so get out there and discover what floats your boat!

Probably the most inspiring message in Jack's talk was the power to believe. Sure, he talked all about exercise and the importance of healthy eating and all of that, but the real tale was the importance of believing in something strongly enough that no matter what anyone tells you, you do what you believe in.

Jack's philosophy in life is "anything in life is possible." And without question, this philosophy has fueled him through all the challenges he faced by preaching the wellness message he so strongly believed in. But unlike what some might think, all those amazing feats Jack performed to generate interest in his message were not about bragging and boasting about Jack -- it was all about getting others to believe that anything is possible, too. If you believe, you will achieve.

Jack's passion is to help others take care of themselves so they too can live a healthy, happy, long life. It's not about him, although he certainly realizes that he has to lead people to this land of wellness by living and breathing the message he preaches. And it's a job he takes very seriously because it works and he knows it because he's helped others believe and achieve it, too!

There's no doubt that Jack and Elaine are motivational speakers, but it's not just all about fitness. They tell stories about how they got started and what it entailed, including all the naysayers who made the journey difficult. But Jack's not a quitter. In fact, all of that probably just motivated him even more. And it worked, so we'll see who gets the last laugh now!

To me, one of the most powerful parts of his presentation was when he told everyone to believe in themselves, and to stop moaning and groaning, and complaining about all the bad things going on in their lives.

"If you believe in something, never give up," Jack said. "Why is it that everyone goes around thinking about all the negative, negative, negative? Think of all the positive things, the wonderful things. We have so much to be grateful for. We live in the greatest country in the world, with so many opportunities, but all people seem to want to talk about are the good 'ole days. They sit around and talk about what's been and what was. Well, the hell with the good 'ole days. We're here in the now and now is what matters most!"

Certainly Jack is appreciative of where we've been as a society and all the improvements we've achieved, but he wants people to move forward and live everyday in the now. We can't worry about all that's already been. We need to go forward in a positive way and look toward tomorrow with a bright future. It doesn't matter how old you are, what matters is living every day to the fullest and taking care of yourself so you can go forward in a healthy, happy, vital way.

Jack believes part of America's problem, with people of all ages frankly (and he's particularly concerned about our youth), is that we're "exceeding the feed limit!" Equally concerning is the fact that we're not moving our bodies. "Inactivity is a killer -- it's not age that makes you old, it's inactivity that makes you old," Jack said.

It takes a lot to be a role model, and particularly when you have to overcome all those who don't believe and want to see you fail. But Jack's a true testament to what can happen if you do, especially when you believe.

Think about living your life as a positive example to others. Start right now, today. It may be the best thing any of us could ever do for ourselves and for others, too.

Art Linkletter, 91

&

Laughter and Living Long

I f laughter plays a role in living longer, then the legendary Art Linkletter, 91, is likely on his way to being one of the longest-lived humans on the planet! And those lucky enough to listen to his message are likely on their way to living a long, happy life too!

There actually is research on the subject of humor and longevity that states the endorphins created and released in the body as the result of laughter contributes to a number of health benefits. In fact, some reports claim that laughter is like internal jogging. And if that's the case, then those experiencing Linkletter's message are likely to do an hour's worth of jogging without ever leaving their chairs.

At a conference where Linkletter gave a keynote address, in his classic, humorous and humble way after hearing his introduction that detailed his amazing accomplishments in 91 years, Linkletter said, "I was worried about half way through that this was an obituary -- surely I was dead!" he laughed. "Although after many wonderful introductions, probably my favorite is still the one given by my 10-year old great-grandson a few years ago who said, 'This is my great-grandfather, he's 80 years old and still alive!'"

Linkletter speaks about seventy times a year, traveling 200K miles, sharing his insight, wisdom and humor to various groups ranging from churches, business executives, education institutes, senior groups, and non-profit organizations around the country. With an extraordinary seventy-year career in the entertainment industry, his television and radio shows, "People Are Funny" and "Kids Say the Darndest Things" are in the record books as two of the longest running shows in broadcast history. He's won an Emmy, a Grammy, recently received the Daytime Emmy Lifetime Achievement Award, has authored 26 books, serves on the Board of Directors of a number of national companies, while also overseeing his many business ventures at Art Linkletter enterprises. He is the recipient of honorary degrees from a number of prestigious Universities, he's also served on many Presidential Councils to address drug abuse and other national issues and was just recently awarded the National Humanities Medal from the President of the United States for his countless contributions.

Family and foundation are important to Linkletter too, who has been married to his wife Lois, for 67 years. He comically shared his family background by saying, "I have nine grandchildren, fifteen great-grandchildren, and five children -- all with the same wife, of course!"

Linkletter seems genuinely appreciative of all he has and believes life should never be taken for granted. "Living is not about just being alive, living is about adventuring, learning new things, discovery, taking risks, and facing life's ups and downs," he said.

Life has not been without tragedy for Linkletter who lost two of his own children, one to a drug overdose and another in an accident.

But Linkletter's a man on a mission and is often referred to as the Ambassador for Positive Living. He turned negatives into positives by reaching out to others facing similar tragedies and believes whole-heartedly in the importance of this approach.

"It's all about attitude. Continuing to make a positive difference and contribution every day," Linkletter said. "My message is really about helping others make the best of the rest of their life, because it's not how old you are -- it's how you are old that really matters."

Linkletter continues to do his life's work and never lets age get in the way of that. He claims he's having the time of his life and when people ask when he plans to retire he says, "To what? I'm doing what I love to do, making a positive difference and enjoying every day!"

Martina Navratilova
&

Love of the Game

Too young to be a legend, but Martina Navratilova, 46, the oldest woman playing on the women's professional tennis tour and the oldest ever titleist at Wimbledon with her recent mixed doubles victory, is a definite hit among fans across the country.

While some may wonder why Martina is still playing, after competing for over 30 years, she said, "The fans response has been so positive. They tell me how inspired they are by what I'm still doing. And I love the game, so why stop?"

But it's more than that. It's also about proving age is just a number, because Martina went on to say that she wouldn't let just age be the determining factor to play or not. She believes she's still competitive and fit enough to continue -- and her court record confirms it.

Yet what actually drives people like Martina to continue 'working' in 'retirement' is the love of what they do. "The tennis ball makes me very happy," she said. And apparently, Navratilova still playing tennis makes others happy, too.

"Martina's amazing and incredibly fit for any age," said Kim Doren, a tennis event spectator. "It's obvious she still loves the sport and is having fun. And she's certainly competitive, so why not? It's inspiring."

At a recent event where Martina was warming up for her match, it was hard to believe there was a 46-year old -- literally twice the age at least, of the other women on the court.

Martina's physique and fitness abilities have obviously played a major role in her ability to continue her high level performance on the court. But it's more than just what's on the outside that makes a true champion, it's what's on the inside and Martina still has what it takes to win. Wisdom, insight and experience are attributes that come with age, and as much as her competitiveness continues to drive her, it is the combination of all these factors that is undoubtedly contributing to Martina's longevity in this sport.

But beyond all the talent and desire, what probably matters most is that Martina genuinely appreciates the joy tennis has brought to her life and is thankful of the gift she's still able to share: the love for the game.

Jhoon Rhee, 71

&

Keeping Life in Balance

I
f you're looking for the secret to being healthy and happy, regardless of age, look no further than within yourself and recognize the role balance plays in your life.

"In order to be healthy, we have to be happy. And in order to be happy, we have to be healthy," said Jhoon Rhee, 71, a world-renown martial arts expert recognized as a national treasure for introducing and popularizing Tae Kwan Do in America, who spoke recently at an AARP National Convention.

Rhee's message is not all about martial arts, but it is about one of the core components of martial arts: self-discipline, which he believes can also lead to other positive life qualities.

In many respects, this is an ageless issue because not only is Rhee recognized as a role model of health and vitality among his peers; he is also highly regarded among today's youth as well. In fact, his martial arts program and philosophy of discipline, respect, and personal responsibility were developed into a curriculum that was adopted by several district elementary schools in Washington, DC. Additionally, Rhee is a legend on Capitol Hill, where he has trained more than 250 members of Congress in Tae Kwon Do, and celebrities like Muhammad Ali and Bruce Lee were also his students.

Rhee's philosophy is ultimately about achieving inner happiness and he believes that by incorporating the martial arts methodology of sound physical fitness with a positive mental attitude, the combination is what really leads to the universal path of freedom, peace, prosperity, and ultimately happiness.

According to Rhee, there are three basic human qualities necessary to be healthy and happy which must be kept in balance: Knowledge in the Mind, Honesty in the Heart, and Strength in the Body.

In daily life, there are various paths people take on the road to happiness, or "happyism," as Rhee calls it. Whether it's doing for others through volunteerism, contributing in some meaningful way through spiritual service, or pursuing our own various goals -- be it training for a gold medal, raising grandchildren, traveling, learning new things, it is the combination of all these things that creates balance in our lives, and therefore enables us to be healthy and happy.

One of the most detrimental things of all is to do nothing with our lives, and particularly as one gets older, to disengage from life -- where one does little more than just exist. The traditional concept of retirement for many consists of pulling out of the workforce and in many ways, pulling out of life. That certainly isn't living. And current studies show there couldn't be anything worse for you. At the same time, there are many healthy, happy retirees who are so busy and engaged; they wonder how they ever had time to work! Rather than sitting around complaining about all the things they can't do anymore, they focus instead on all the things they still can do and get to it. That's living -- and age has nothing to do with that.

How is it that those who have nothing are happier than those who seem to have everything and are still miserable? What matters most is what's on the inside of our being -- and that's something we can all control.

Rhee believes living his life as an example to others is one of the most effective forms of teaching. Certainly lifestyle, discipline, and balance are at the core. He eats healthily, including drinking water, juices and Korean tea, and he eats at least five bananas a day as well as grapes, peaches and other fruit. During meals, he piles heaps of vegetables on his plate and only eats fish or chicken on occasion, and beef on rare occasion. Rhee doesn't smoke or drink and does his best to avoid sugar.

Rhee's exercise regimen is equally impressive. He still does 1,000 push-ups a day and he hasn't missed his daily 2-hour workout in 17 years! He has the flexibility of a 10-year old and claims he's in better shape today than he was 20 years ago. Now, that's a tribute to discipline!

Combined with his continued contributions in teaching his philosophy to people of all ages, his love of music, people, and a desire to always keep learning, it's really no surprise that Rhee is healthy and happy -- because he keeps life in balance.

"Everybody wants to be happy," Rhee said. But it doesn't have anything to do with how old you are. The key to a healthy, happy life is keeping everything in balance."

Governor Ann Richards, 70

&othergo;

The Ageless Spirit Secret

We've all met those seemingly ageless people who just keep on keeping on. Often at a pace few of us ever maintained, let alone later in life, and we wonder what the secret is. Ann Richards, the spunky septuagenarian, former Governor of Texas, is one of those breeds, and she shared her insights with me recently.

It's likely Richards has been a fireball most of her life. She's a woman on a mission and although her missions change as she journeys down the road of life, this is a passionate, intelligent, insightful woman who likely never went at a snails pace and has shown no sign of slowing down since leaving the governor's mansion in 1995.

Richards divides her time between Austin, TX and New York where she currently serves as a senior advisor at a consulting firm that helps companies analyze, develop and implement their public agenda. She began her distinguished career as a junior high school teacher, but was always a political activist who went on to serve the people of Texas as a county commissioner, state treasurer and finally, as the state's 45th governor. Richards is a member or serves on the board of several corporations as well as philanthropic, education and public interest groups.

While she admits she may be "ready to retire and shut it down a bit," in the same breath she also says with a laugh, "But I'm not going to slow down until Willard Scott (the CBS-TV news member who lists 100-yr old birthdays) puts my name up on that TV screen!"

It's evident Richards' sense of humor has been a key component in her life, along with her desire to make a positive difference -- which has likely been the fuel that keeps her going. Her most recent book, "*I'm Not Slowing Down*," is the account of her battle with osteoporosis and is an effort to encourage other women to start taking better care of themselves.

To say Richards looks great is an understatement. But more importantly, she feels great and claims she's healthier today at 70, than she has ever been.

"When I realized I was actually going to live long enough to collect Social Security, I started taking better care of myself because I plan to collect every dime I paid into that system!" Richards laughed. "Now that I do all those good things to take care of myself, I'm afraid I'm going to live longer than I may want to!"

Women's health is a personal mission for Richards who remembers painstakingly watching her mother "break off in pieces" from osteoporosis and vowed she would make something positive out of that experience.

"I was adamant and motivated to make sure that didn't happen to me because I didn't want my kids to suffer through watching me go the way Mama went," Richards said.

Richards' osteoporosis diagnosis came in 1996, after she tripped on some gravel while out on a walk with her youngest daughter.

"I put my hand down to support my fall and ended up breaking two bones instead," Richards remembered. "With the combination of my Mama's condition and this, it was time to get serious about osteoporosis education for all of us."

Osteoporosis is a disease in which the bones become extremely porous and brittle, break easily and heal slowly. Women can lose upward of 30 percent of the bone mass in their spine within the first five years after menopause. But it's not just a women's issue, twenty percent of men are also diagnosed with osteoporosis.

While often considered a natural part of aging, it doesn't have to be debilitating, and that's the message Richards is adamant about sharing.

"Once I was diagnosed, I made the necessary lifestyle changes to control it instead of it controlling me," Richards said. "I got on a regimen of regular workouts, healthy eating, and medication. Then, four years later I tripped again, but this time I didn't break a thing."

Richards admits her lifestyle likely contributed to her osteoporosis. "I smoked like a stove and drank like a fish earlier in my life and studies now show that alcohol inhibits the construction of new bone cells and smoking adds 10 years to the age of your bones, while also reducing the body's ability to absorb calcium."

While most associate aging with negative changes, Richards looks at life these stages with a refreshing perspective.

"We've all heard about the 'change of life' ladies, when we get all hot and crazy, thinking we're approaching the end of life and that we're all doomed," Richards said. "Frankly, it use to be that women were put here to reproduce and once that stops, we're considered 'out of business'. But honey, many of us were out of that business long before menopause!" she laughed. "I'm here to tell you that in actuality, menopause is the opening curtain on a highly entertaining second act of life. In fact, I started my second phase running for Governor!"

While Richards' glass is definitely half full versus half empty, she also admits to being an adoring grandma of seven grandchildren. "Most of them are really cute," she said. But she's also very clear on the fact that she is not a baby-sitter.

"I like to see them, and I like them to come visit me -- invitation only -- stay a couple of hours and then that's it!" she said.

She knows what matters most and that's the here and now, family and friends, and new adventures. Maybe down the road she'll learn to ride the Harley she got for her 60th birthday that she's just been to busy to ride.

One thing's for sure, Richards loves life and believes it's what we make of it that really matters.

"It's the only life we're going to get so don't put it off -- live it and love it!"

That just may be the ageless spirit secret.

Pancho Segura, 80

ॐ

Still Loves The Game

T hey say if you live long enough and you're one of the great ones, you become a legend. Certainly this is the case for Pancho Segura, the 80 year-young, jovial, tennis master who toured for nearly two decades and is one of the most prominent figures in the history of the sport. His entry into the Hall of Fame in 1984 confirms his role as one of the all time greats.

But it wasn't always easy for Segura, and the sport was nothing like it is today. Yet there are certain qualities that transcend time and circumstances that are virtually ageless. It is these things that have contributed to the drive he has inside, which made it all happen and continues to guide him today. Frankly it has little to do with tennis, it's actually a lesson about life.

I hooked up with Francisco Olegario "Pancho" Segura at the legendary La Costa Resort & Spa, where he is somewhat of a fixture after spending 25 years there as the Pro and Director of Tennis after retiring from the men's professional circuit.

Although retired from competitive play, Segura will never retire from life. He still loves the game -- of life, as well as tennis. This passion serves as his foundation from which good things have come - and it hasn't changed much over time so it's easy to say this has nothing to do with age.

"I don't worry about my age," Segura said. "I love life, so as long as I'm still here, I'm going to enjoy it to the fullest by always looking forward and being appreciative for what has been."

It is undoubtedly this spirit that has enabled him to overcome some of the challenges he's faced, which actually began at a very young age. Born and raised in Ecuador, Segura suffered a childhood attack of rickets, which deformed his legs, but not his will, and also led him to the sport of tennis.

"There's always a silver-lining if you just look for it," Segura remembered, looking back on his condition. "Since I was too small and weak for most of the other sports, the doctors suggested I take up tennis to help improve my conditioning. As it turned out, I turned my weakness into an advantage by being one of the first to ever utilize a two-fisted forehand! I was so weak that I had to grip the racket with both hands and as it stands now, that method has become one of the most successful aspects of the game."

With that same will, drive, and determined spirit he still exemplifies today, Segura pounced on the sport, overcoming his seemingly physical limitations from his childhood condition and won his native Ecuadorian title at 17 in 1938, along with various other Latin American tennis titles. He made a big impression when he first appeared on the North American tennis scene in 1941. Although somewhat of a curious sight, he made up in mite with his jarring strokes and jovial personality. A big smile and a yen for the battle proved to be the tools he needed to overcome what first appeared to be disadvantages: an unorthodox two-fisted forehand, flimsy-looking bowed legs and a 5-foot-6 frame. Yet these very weaknesses became his strengths. His footwork was admirable; he was quick, nimble, and extremely effective. Within a year he had a #4 U.S. ranking.

"It just goes to show that it's all about heart -- the will to survive and overcome adversity," Segura said. "Whether it's tennis or other aspects of life, you've gotta go for it and take on the challenge."

Not only did Segura become one of the crowd favorites with his hardy, good-natured personality always on the ready with a smile and a joke, he was also a fierce competitor who later became one of the most well respected coaches in the game.

Perhaps of his most famous accomplishments was his coaching role to Jimmy Connors, believed by many to be one of the greatest tennis players ever. Segura is also well known for having one of the sharpest minds in the game, yet he'll tell you that strategy is only good if it's executed.

"The thing I liked best about Jimmy, who I started coaching at age 16 after my playing career was over, was he too proved that the little guys can make it as long as we've got the big heart," Segura said. "You've got to have talent, there's no question about that, but you've also got to want it and be willing to do what it takes to get it and that's usually what separates the greats."

Today, Segura still attacks life much like he did the net. His priorities are his health, family, and continuing to contribute to his profession. Somewhat of an ambassador to the game, he still travels to most of the Grand Slam events including the Australian Open, the French, and he even sits in the Royal box at Wimbledon and the Presidential box at the U.S. Open.

Although he has arthritis and virtually no cartilage left in his knees, he's out walking his three miles daily at 5 AM and believes this routine has kept him fairly pain free. He stretches too, and continues to play doubles a few times a week. He's happily married to his wife of 40 years, Beverley, who keeps them both healthy by focusing on a mostly non-fat diet, but Segura admits he still likes his daily glass of wine or vodka to wind down the day.

But what one really notices about Segura comes from his spirit inside. He twinkles, with a laugh and smile that is contagious and heart-warming. Probably hanging out with comedians like Dean Martin, Mel Brooks, Rob Reiner, and Milton Berle, contributed to his sense of humor and love to laugh, but Pancho also believes enjoying life is a secret to his longevity.

"I love life to the fullest, always have and suspect I always will," he said. "It's my spirit, the desire to enjoy life and always look at it with the glass half full versus half empty. Life is precious and in many ways much like a tennis match: if you give up on life, you lose. But if you attack the net and go for life's gusto, victory is sweet."

John Wooden, 93

ॐ

A Coach's Life Lessons

T he term 'legend' is usually used to describe entities who have been around a while, but what's often more important, is what they leave behind.

Coach John Wooden, 93, who many know as the 'Wizard of Westwood' for his amazing accolades as coach of the UCLA Bruin basketball team, is certainly a legend who will indeed leave a legacy. But it's not about his achievements; it's rather the lessons he's taught through example and the lives he's influenced that may be what really matters most.

Believe it or not, Wooden doesn't consider himself a coach, even though he's in the history books, the Hall of Fame and was chosen by ESPN as "Basketball's Coach of the Century." He's a teacher, and definitely one we can all learn from.

Not surprising, the secrets of success he is recognized for implementing on the basketball court are easily transferable, as they are in reality, lessons for life.

It's obvious he believes strongly in the importance of learning. A couple of his favorite quotes are, "It's what you learn after you know it all that really counts," and "When I'm through learning, I'm through."

Wooden, who has been teaching for over 70 years, is still at it today because he loves to teach. It's easy to see why his success principles transfer from the hard court to the boardroom because it's all about helping others learn to be the best they can be, regardless who they are or what they do.

"There's nothing more important than striving to help others," Wooden said. "Yet in today's 'me society,' it seems we often lose sight of that."

Wooden has never lost sight of what's important and will tell you that the real trophies are not the hardware on the mantle, but instead are the people and the lives they lead and the positive differences they make to the planet that really counts.

His philosophy of success is having peace of mind, which he believes is a direct result of self satisfaction in knowing you've made the effort to do your best at becoming the best you can possible be. He's also clear to point out that it's not about being better than someone else, but rather never ceasing to be the best you can be.

Considered by many as the greatest coach in the history of sports, or at least basketball, some found his lack of scouting during the off-season rather strange. But Wooden had a logical explanation that is congruent with his success philosophy.

"I didn't need to focus on what other teams were doing," Wooden stated. "All I needed to be concerned with was helping our team be the best they could be and let the results speak for themselves."

But of all the things that matter most, Wooden says it's faith, family and friends, for these were the priorities instilled in him by his parents, and ones he hopes he passes along to others.

It's obvious he walks the talk because when asked what is his most prized possession, Wooden, without hesitation, described a 90th birthday gift from his granddaughter who assembled a collection of family pictures into a book with the inscription stating she hoped to meet a man as wonderful as him some day.

So while some are out there worrying about making a living by what they get, what really matters is making life by what you give. Wooden gives lessons for a lifetime.

SUPER SENIORS

෪

Walt Bailey, 90

&

Feeling Good By Giving

W alt Bailey, 90, is one of those wonderful beings that make a positive difference on our planet by taking care of others. Always has, always will. And he suspects it must be in his genes because it's definitely part of his being.

"My wife, Eloise, calls me a professional volunteer and we laugh about the idea that I'm possibly missing a gene, the "just say no" one!" Walt laughed. "But I think I must have

been destined to give because I grew up helping others and have just continued it all my life."

There are countless beneficiaries of Walt's giving -- from family to strangers, businesses and non-profit groups and just about everything in between. In fact, when stray cats start adopting you, you begin to wonder if maybe you do have a special gift of caring for others that even animals recognize, too.

"This pretty little calico cat just appeared one day out of no where and decided this was going to be home," Walt remembered. "Nobody recognized her so I of course took her in and named her 'Boots.' She follows me everywhere. And she even sits, shakes, and rolls over on command! She's definitely become a fun, furry friend."

Not only does Walt have a special way with animals, but it's with people too. He has an innate ability and desire to make others happy and says that it's the joy he sees in others that inspires him to keep on giving.

Being from a close-knit family, Walt was actively involved in Boy Scouts with his sons and even stayed on with the program for several years even after his sons had already left. He was a Search & Rescue volunteer for over 30 years, and is one of the founders of General Dynamics' retiree club (who he worked for as a tool engineer for over 30 years). For the past 31 years, he has volunteered at UCSD Hospital -- 23 years in the Emergency Room, and the last 8 years as a "Cuddler" for premature babies and infants with medical problems.

As much joy as this brings him, Walt is certainly not immune to his own challenges, which actually makes his giving that much more special. He is the primary caregiver for his wife who was diagnosed with Alzheimers over ten years

ago. And with no children or other family living in the area,
this is a duty he takes on willingly and lovingly, just like all
his other giving activities.

"I think it's a healthy occupation to be a giver," Walt
shared. "When you give, you feel good, and I think it pro-
motes good health, too. I've always believed in the body/mind
connection -- how we think affects how we feel. So feeling
good by giving may be contributing to my living a healthy,
long life."

It obviously would be easier to just sit back and take
care of his own things, but Walt says he'd feel incomplete if
he didn't give. He wouldn't know what to do with himself. In
many ways, he says his accepting of the way things are and
his volunteering are his respite that enables him to feel his
efforts help others and are therefore beneficial.

Walt Bailey's giving does make a difference. And if it
feels good -- do it!

Irene Bann, 97

ðﬂ

Eighty Years On the Job

I rene Bann, 97, has worked longer than some people have lived   almost eight decades! She started her professional career with the firm now known as Smith Barney, on October 26, 1926 and decided her last day would appropriately be October 29, 2004, seventy-eight years on the job and the 75th anniversary of "Black Tuesday," one of the most memorable days in the history of the stock market.

Irene's career has also been memorable, but in a good way. She was 19 and the very first woman to work at H. Hentz & Company, where she started as a typist and assistant telephone operator -- back in the day when being a telephone operator meant juggling multiple calls and a complicated switchboard -- no easy voice mail systems like we have today.

When WWII came along, Irene, like so many other women around the world, took on new responsibilities and opportunities. Irene handled operations for the office, and was certainly capable of doing so as she was also a graduate of Miami Jacobs Business College.

Not long after successfully handling this new position, Irene went on to obtain her Securities license and became a full-time registered representative.

Irene persevered through countless company mergers, take-overs, name changes -- and likely more retirement parties than she'd like to count, just never her own. She kept keeping on every day because "there was a job to do and I did it," Irene said.   "I never really thought about retiring. Nor did I ever feel any pressure to retire. I do remember the company giving me a nice 'longevity party' when I was 75 or 80, but it wasn't my retirement -- I wasn't done yet."

Irene admits she's enjoyed her work routine but she's also looking forward to not going to work, for a change. "After 78 years and now only a couple of days retired, I must admit it feels pretty good so far," Irene said. "I'll miss the people I suspect, but I'm ready for a new adventure -- something different.

Irene plans to move in with her niece about 150 miles away and is looking forward to exploring her new town -- by car because yes, she does still drive. "I plan to investigate the area -- drive around and familiarize myself with all the streets and where things are," she said.

Of course, for Irene, it's always been about the journey. When asked her thoughts on aging, she directly stated, "Well, you really can't categorize it (aging) as being a certain way or thing because each person is different as an individual, so what they choose to do and their perspective will be unique to them. It (aging) can't be considered a curse because it's just as natural as getting on a train -- going along to your destination."

How long Irene will live, she has no idea. Her Mom, however, lived to 100 and so far it seems Irene's on pace to match that. She readily admits she doesn't have any special secret to longevity but does believe moderation is key.

"I think everything in moderation is important," Irene said. "Just do what's normal. It never occurred to me to drink too much or overeat because I always felt so uncomfortable when I did that. It just didn't make sense to do those things, so I didn't. Seems that when you do do those things, maybe that's where the health problems begin. It's all about moderation -- just do what's normal and enjoy life. It's turned out pretty good for me so far."

Although she worked beyond what's 'normal' for some, Irene enjoyed it and that's probably more important than how long she worked. Bottom line: this is what worked for her and she hopes her advice will work for others too.

Pat & Meta Brazell

&

The Dynamic Duo

W ith one foot on the running board and a hat on my head, I'm always ready to go!" said 99-year young Meta Brazell, long-time resident of Lakeside. Ever since I've known Meta, and her delightful daughter, Pat Brazell, 78, I've always referred to them as the "dynamic duo" due to their endless commitment to community service and volunteer activities.

"It all started with my love for driving, actually," laughed Meta. "I was helping one of my daughters who volunteered for the city, but had a broken leg and needed a chauffeur to help shuffle her about to various activities. Being that I loved to drive, I was happy to oblige. It was great to see and learn about all the different community programs. In fact, I enjoyed it so much I decided to sign up and be part of it too!"

She's been a part of it alright. Meta's won so many volunteer awards, she's lost count! Some of the organizations she's affiliated with include the American Cancer Society, Alzheimer's Association, AARP, the local Historical Society, Aging and Independence Services (AIS), and the list goes on and on and on.

But it's definitely a family affair because daughter Pat is equally involved and she too, has won bunches of awards. Pat currently serves as the AARP community coordinator and provides all sorts of booklets and information at local health fairs, corporate programs, etc.

"We really do make a wonderful team," Pat shared. "It sure keeps us both going and it's a nice feeling to be helping others."

Meta strongly believes that keeping on the go and having someplace to be has contributed to her longevity. But she also believes there are other factors, too.

"A sense of humor is of the utmost importance," Meta said. "And so is family, so I feel pretty blessed to have them both. Laughter has always been a big part of our family. We have fun together and if something doesn't go right, we try to find some humor in it somehow and believe it's important to be able to laugh at ourselves."

Having a positive spirit has undoubtedly also contributed to their longevity. And when you look at these two, you'd guess they're both twenty years younger than their actual age.

"We all have aches and pains -- that's just a part of living this long," Meta said. "But I don't see the benefit in complaining about it because doesn't everyone our age have a few problems? Maybe complaining is a release for some people. I guess I'd just rather think about more positive things. Now that certainly doesn't mean I'm not sympathetic to those who have health problems. I have them too, I just don't have much tolerance for them, so I just choose to spend my time trying to forget about them and find the best way to do that is by keeping myself busy and my mind involved in other things."

Of course, when you get to be the age of 99, there are all sorts of other things you can think about -- like what kind of fun you're going to plan for birthday parties. For her 90th

birthday she got to hold the Cup -- America's Cup, that is.
She had a party planned at the Yacht Club and it was shortly
after Dennis Conner had won the America's Cup yachting
race, bringing the prestigious trophy back to the United States,
and more specifically to his hometown club.

"They literally had a chain around that cup, and me
too, when they surprised me and brought it to our party,"
remembered Meta. "That was quite a thrill because I'd never
been in chains before, so at the age of 90 it's was indeed a
first!"

But for Meta it was her 99th birthday celebration that
was perhaps the most special. She'd always wanted to see the
Great Wall of China and not only did she see it -- she went
right up on it.

"It was an absolute thrill and even more beautiful than
I ever could have imagined," Meta said. "My grandson works
in China so he made all sorts of special arrangements for us
that made the trip incredibly special. We had our own inter-
preter, driver, and even a birthday cake and beautiful roses in
our hotel suite."

One thing Meta specifically remembers about her journey was the response to her by the people of China. This is a
country that reveres elders and anyone with white hair is considered an icon.

"You should have seen Mom -- surrounded by children
and all sorts of people," Pat remembered. "But the children
were particularly fascinated by her, especially her wrinkles!"

"Yes, that was quite funny," Meta laughed. "I guess
they had never really seen wrinkles before because the older
people there have a different skin type that just doesn't seem
to wrinkle the way ours does. So the kids wanted to touch my

face and feel what it was like. They did so with gentleness, but with lots of giggles too!"

Of course, Meta and Pat feel right at home with laughter, and with children too. Between the two of them, Pat has eight grandchildren and eight great-grandchildren, which means those are great- and great-great grandchildren to Meta. In fact, there are thirty-five family members just here locally, and this five-generation family also regularly attends their church picnics, too.

"Pretty soon we'll have three generations living under one roof," Pat shared. "Mom and I are getting a new roommate. My daughter will be joining us and we can't wait because that will mean three-times the fun!"

And when you talk to Meta about what she credits her long life to she never misses the chance for a laugh. "Well just the other day we had leftover cheesecake and pizza for breakfast, do you think that's the secret?" Meta laughed.

Probably not, but what probably does contribute is her fabulously positive spirit, her terrific sense of humor, and her overall outlook on life. Meta also thinks volunteering has made a significant difference in her life, and always encourages other retirees to get out and do the same.

Meta likes a little TV now and then too -- Jeopardy is her absolute favorite evening show. And when I asked if she liked to watch, "Who Wants To Be a Millionaire?" she said she did, but then we both agreed that if she could just figure out what the real secret was for her living such a long and happy life -- she'd bottle it and then she'd be the millionaire!

Brisbane, Australia

&

Life's A Journey

L ife is about the journey, not the destination. But in this case, I want to share an experience to an extraordinary destination, Brisbane, Australia, where we traveled to attend the 14th Annual World Veteran Track & Field Championships.

But this is not about Australia as a destination; it's about the experience of the journey. This was a gathering of 6,000 "master" athletes (all over the age of 40), representing 79 countries from all over the world -- 1,000 of which were over the age of 65. Few of them ever imagined they'd be competing in world sport competition at this stage in their lives, but all of them seemed to be there for the same reason -- and it wasn't about winning medals. It was about the camaraderie and the new challenges these games provided that fueled these folks -- and it was inspiring to watch.

Of course, these championships do provide the opportunity to demonstrate some pretty incredible athleticism and physical fitness abilities, but I witnessed more than just that going on. I spent most of my time following the over age 75 group, because they re the ones who generally face the most challenges -- physically, as well as mentally, and even emotionally, as they fight the mindset issues, which can often be more of a barrier than anything.

Some of you may be wondering why any 75 to 100 year-old man or woman would even want to compete in a track and field event. But it s perhaps this very aspect -- the non-physical part, which really enables these people to do the things many consider impossible at any age, let alone in these later stages of life. They are an exceptional breed, but it's actually their beliefs and internal spirit that really drives them to do what they do. They honestly believe age is just a number and it's certainly not going to stop them from continuing to live their life, experience new adventures, and challenge themselves.

For example, Les Amey of Brisbane, Australia, the event's oldest competitor at 101, competed in the 100m Sprints and the 1500m run! In addition to setting a world-record in each event, he also had his own private fan club: Connie Gibson, age "100.5" and Louise Russell, 103, both members of Queensland's 100+ Club! Although he didn't blister the track with much more than a high-speed shuffle, the fact that he was out there doing it -- and actually enjoying it as he smiled from start to finish, was the inspiring part. After he was finished, he sat down for a rest with the ladies and chatted away while they all enjoyed some tea and cookies!

Rosario Rocha Iglesias, of Mexico City, was the oldest female competitor at 91. Nicknamed, "Chayito" which means little one in Spanish (she stands little more than four feet tall), was equally inspiring. She competed in the 200m sprints, the 800m and the 1500m run. She too, set world records in both the 800m and 1500m. In fact, this was the first time a 90-year young woman has ever even run the 800m in world competition and she did it rather impressively, with a time under seven minutes!

Rosario has a flaming spirit. She's been an entrepreneur for over 60 years, running her own newspaper stand near Aztec Stadium downtown, even delivering many clients' papers -- some in which she still does today. She's only been competing since she was 80, at which time she told her family she'd like to learn how to run after witnessing many marathons pass by her stand, which is what initially sparked her interest in the sport. She's become a national hero in Mexico, and likely all over the world by now. All the athletes wanted pictures with her and she was featured in every newspaper and television news broadcast.

Whatever she's doing, she's apparently doing it right because she claims to have no health problems, aches or pains. She says she eats whatever she wants, although not much meat, but she does enjoy her Coca-Cola. Her daily workout consists mostly of walking, and running her newsstand. But her Grandson, Conrado Peralta, also coaches her about 20 minutes a day with a stretching and jogging routine. Family is a priority in Rocha's life and with 15 grandchildren, 30 great-grandchildren, 5 great-great-grandchildren and 2 great-great-great grandchildren; you can imagine how the celebrations become major fiestas!

On the USA home front, we can all be proud to salute Bert Morrow, 88, who competed in the 100m and 200m Sprints, as well as the 80m Hurdles. Being a world-record holder in the hurdles and somewhat of an ambassador for American track and field, Bert had some stiff competition, particularly considering he had to race against some of the 'young-buck' 85-, 86-, and even 87-year-olds in his division. But he performed like a champ, making it into the finals for both the 100m and 200m sprints, and winning the silver medal in the hurdles -- just barely missing the gold by a few seconds to an 85-year old from Finland!

The real story however, was that Bert had been injured for six months coming into the competition. He rarely talked about it because he didn't want to sound like he was making excuses, but as a gerontologist who knows the challenges of competing at this age, let alone while recovering from an injury, what he accomplished is beyond any gold medal. Although he continued his workout routine as best he could during the time leading up to this championship, his therapist really only released him as "ready to go" the day before we left for Australia.

Bert continued his stretching regimen, but obviously was unable to perform his usual workout the way he normally would. When the time came to run the 100m and 200m sprints, there was deep competition, and although he favored his injured leg a bit (likely saving himself for the hurdles), he still made it into the finals. Even though he didn't win a medal, being in the finals is a victory in itself with the tough competition -- not to mention coming away from both races without an injury!

But the real story was the hurdles -- an amazing example of athleticism, especially following a six month injury. The morning of the race he still hadn't taken a practice leap and decided he was just going to "go for it and put it on automatic pilot," Bert said.

Bert and I have been friends for years, so to say I was a bit nervous is an understatement. But to describe the pride I felt as he flew down the track, not touching one single hurdle and getting to the finish line with his body in tact, just barely being squeaked out of the gold medal by a mere 5 seconds, brought tears to my eyes and the audience to their feet!

All these athletes give it everything they've got and it takes more than just physical fitness to do what these people do. It takes pride and drive, and that's what keeps the spirit alive, regardless of age. It's not about winning and the medals -- that's the destination. It's about the journey and how to keep going every day in this game we call life.

Mary Davis, 65

&

Black Belt Gals

I t's not unusual to see a black belt hanging in most women's closets. But for one family, there are three black belts -- and we're not talking fashion here, we're talking karate.

To say it's a family affair is no understatement for this mother and two-daughter black belt team who got their start by observing a karate class one of the granddaughters was taking. "Initially we got hooked on Karate as a good form of exercise while we were watching the class," said Mary Davis, 65. "My granddaughter was the first to try it and when my daughter Debbie found out there was an adult class, she signed up. Next thing I know, I'm observing Debbie's class and thought it looked great so I signed up too."

Mary admits that at first she thought she might be too old to take on karate, but after talking with Sensei (the Japanese term for teacher) Kikuchi, he encouraged her to give it a try and she's never looked back.

Although Mary recognizes being a black belt in Karate is an unusual endeavor, it's an accomplishment she's proud of because it was never anything she ever dreamed of doing.

"I always thought martial arts to be kind of violent, but it's so much more than just the physical aspects; it teaches you about self control, discipline, confidence and so much more. I'm amazed at all I've learned and how I've stuck with it to achieve this level and now be teaching too," Mary said.

Mary and Debbie went through the process first and kept each other motivated. They took classes twice a week and after four years and 12 belt levels, they were ready to go for their black belts. The other daughter Julie, followed in their footsteps shortly thereafter.

"We never started this with the intention of getting our black belts," Mary remembered. "We were just looking for a good exercise class we could stick with and one thing lead to another. As it turned out, I got my black belt for my 60th birthday!"

The three-day black belt testing is "grueling" according to Mary, and there were no allocations made for her age. The first day consists of performing the basic forms and movements, the second day is sparring and the third day is endurance, including running, sit-ups, stair climbing, and more.

"Sensei Kikuchi has been a great role model who never let my age be a deterrent," Mary said. "I am the oldest, yes, but the Asian culture reveres and respects age. And now as a second degree black belt, I teach both a martial arts and adult fitness class and all my students are younger than I am."

Mary's martial arts life has provided countless benefits ranging from self-defense techniques to improved flexibility and upper body strength to better endurance, less arthritis pain and a recently impressive bone density test result.

"There will be no apple sauce days for me-I'm going to be the oldest woman doing karate!" Mary claimed.

And, yes, Mary can break boards with a simple karate chop.

Andelina Dominguez

&

Living to 115

S econd-by-second, minute-by-minute, hour-by-hour, no matter who you are or where you are - with every tick of the clock, we're all getting older. Even though our individual journeys will vary from person to person, we're all on the trip of a lifetime -- an incredible journey -- where the longer you live, the more of life you experience. So imagine, if you can, the trip of living to 115, as Andelina Dominguez did.

Born February 19, 1887 in the Cape Verde Islands (off west Africa), Andelina lived in three centuries and is in the record books as one of the oldest people in the world.

Living to the age of 100 is quite an extraordinary feat, yet not as uncommon today as it once was. In 1960, there were only 3K centenarians -- today there are more than 65K, according to recent census reports.

But for those looking for a single secret to living a century or more, there may be some disappointment because there doesn't appear to be one. The good news however, is there are likely several contributing factors ranging from healthy lifestyles and friendship to genetics and medical breakthroughs.

Currently, some of the most exciting aging research centers on living long. While it's estimated that one in three girls born today will see their 100th birthday, studies also show that a sibling living to 100 dramatically increases the chances another sibling will celebrate a centenarian birthday, too.

In Andelina's case, all of her eleven brothers and sisters lived into their 90s and 100s, according to her grandson. But at the same time, Andelina outlived all of her four children, the eldest died at age 70.

With genetics reportedly playing only a 30% role in determining how long we live, perhaps we should pay more attention to the 70% majority role lifestyle plays and therefore, the control we have over our aging process. What we do, what we eat and what we think can affect not only how long we live, but perhaps more importantly, how well we live -- our quality of life. While it's exciting to see the increase in longevity, we also need to consider the importance of not only our life expectancy, but our health expectancy as well -- the proportion of our life that's spent feeling healthy.

Believe it or not, Andelina was in remarkably good health and didn't take a single medication. She was healthy, alert, animated, feisty, and get this -- her hair hadn't even turned fully gray. Andelina didn't credit Clairol in a bottle, rather she believed one of her secrets to living long was actually never having been to the beauty parlor! Additionally she credited her strong faith in God, never drinking, smoking, or playing cards as other contributors.

Andelina lived in her own home and was cooking family dinners every Sunday night up to the age of 107 and was walking ably until the age of 110.

"She'd never been in the hospital that we know of and she'd never really been sick to my knowledge," said a family friend. "She was just full of life and quite a remarkable woman."

Andelina's longevity exemplifies an incredible journey and should be encouraging news to us all as we embark upon this new phase of aging.

Shirley Klein, 64 & Celia, 96

&⁓

Ageless Friendship

S hirley, 64, was on her way to fix her friend's computer when I bumped into her at the gym the other day. She wanted to be sure they'd be able to communicate over the next few months while Shirley was out of the country on a sailing sabbatical. Then they were going to enjoy a friendly workout together -- but this was a mental workout with the game of Scrabble -- and Shirley's pal is Ceila, 96.

For those who might be wondering what a 64 and 96-year old would have in common to develop such a strong friendship, take a look at some of your own treasured friends and ask yourself whether age ever comes into the equation when making friendship choices. Hopefully your answer is no -- and frankly, research shows that there are actually benefits of having both older and younger friends -- so here we are again asking that familiar question, what's age got to do with it?

Shirley had told me about Ceila before, and I'd always wanted to meet her. Now, after my initial meeting and obser-vance of their special relationship, I can see why the two have stayed connected...and will continue to do so over months and miles.

"She stimulates me," Shirley claimed of Ceila. "She's engaging -- bright, interesting, witty, funny, and one heck-of-a

Scrabble player -- she beats me routinely and I swear I really am trying to win!" Shirley laughed.

Their relationship started as a professional one, seven years ago, when Shirley started teaching a strength training exercise class at the retirement community where Ceila lives. Although the workout component is an essential part of any exercise class, most participants will tell you that the social element is equally important -- meeting new people, making friends, and genuinely caring about each other.

Shirley and Ceila's story is no different. Although it's been almost two years since Shirely has taught there, their friendship has grown ever stronger, even though they no longer have their exercise workout in common. As is typical with many new friendships, Shirley and Ceila met by having one thing in common, yet over time they discovered they actually shared many other interests which have contributed to the special relationship they share today.

"Shirley is such a giving person," Ceila shared. "She cares so much about people and she's truly a joy to be around. I learn a lot from Shirley."

On this recent visit, it was as much about spending some special time together before Shirely set sail for six months, as it was about making sure she fixed Ceila's computer so the two could stay connected via email. Apparently during their last visit, Shirley inadvertently did something to Ceila's system and Ceila was anxious to get her computer back in working order. Imagine that, a 96-year young recognizing something was amiss with her system -- and equally impressive, a 64-year young friend who could fix it!

When we arrived, Ceila was already challenging herself with the newspaper's daily "Word Jumble" and quickly recruited Shirley and me to assist her with one that was way beyond both our capabilities. We all sat and played with it for a bit before finally giving up after Ceila chimed in and said, "Well, we'll just have to wait to learn until tomorrow's paper gives us the answer!"

After a brief chat about the country's current events, including a quick review of the Sunday New York Times -- which Shirley brings to Ceila each week, it was on to tackle the Macintosh. Although Ceila says she doesn't go on-line that much, she does use her computer to correspond with her niece in France, as well as other family and friends from around the globe.

"Having friends and people to communicate with is one of the most important things in life," Ceila shared. "But as you get older, it seems more difficult to keep in contact with people. The telephone becomes a challenge because hearing dissipates, writing gets a bit tricky to do and read, and even the computer can be a bit overwhelming to learn initially. But even with my fading eyesight, I can still see the screen's large print and the stimulation it provides is well worth the effort."

Stimulation is a key element to aging well and is undoubtedly another reason why this ageless friendship works. Although we all recognize the importance of stimulation, the challenge often lies in finding others who share the same interests.

"It seems harder to make friends later in life," Ceila said. "But loneliness is even worse, at any age. We get all caught up in our own routines and just don't realize how much more enjoyable life can be when it's shared with others. Friendships take time to develop. They evolve over time, which can actually be a wonderful journey if people would just give it a chance."

Although Ceila and Shirley have developed a mutually beneficial friendship which has expanded beyond their initial meeting in exercise class, it was one common link that began a chain reaction that has now evolved into something beyond either one of their expectations.

"It feels more like peers -- not a generational gap," Shirley said. "And the wisdom this woman shares, that can frankly only come with age, is probably what I love most."

Although both admit they've always been interested in people -- and are probably happiest when they're around people to share, laugh and be with -- get out of the way when that Scrabble game comes out because no one stands a chance when these two battle the board!

Bert Morrow, 92

℘

Healthy Hurdles

Bert Morrow has faced his share of life's hurdles over the 92 years he's been on the planet. But as a world-record track and field hurdler who didn't even run his first hurdle until the age of 69, there were many who thought he was crazy taking up such a demanding sport at an age when most are starting to slow down. Who would have known that on his 20th anniversary of hurdling, the sport that some thought just might kill him -- may actually have saved his life.

Overcoming challenges has been a part of life for Bert. Both his parents died early, without Bert ever really knowing his father. And although he had more time with his mother, for the most part, Bert was raised by his grandparents who taught him through example that age is just a number and living life every day to its fullest is really the ultimate goal.

"I've been lucky, it's just that simple," Bert said. "I guess I'm suppose to still be here because I've certainly been through enough 'close calls' to know that there must be some reason why I'm still here. So as long as I can continue to contribute in some way, then I'm happy to do so."

Bert has made his share of contributions including serving five years in the Royal Navy as a commander of torpedo boats in the English Channel during WWII, then as a top executive for General Motors. Since retirement, he's been an example to others on the importance of staying healthy and active with age, which also landed him a 3-year stint on national television as the 'Chiquita Banana Man' -- featuring Bert running hurdles, breaking world-records in his 80s, and starting every morning with his 'Breakfast of Champions' grains/cereal recipe, topped with a banana, of course!

"I'll never forget the day I got the call from Chiquita," Bert recalled. "Before the man ever introduced himself, the first and only thing he wanted to know was whether or not I ate bananas," Bert laughed. "I said, well of course I eat bananas, don't be silly, who is this anyway? Guess it was just meant to be."

Bert is without question an inspiration to all who meet him. He fascinates people -- particularly with his age, his story and his "joie de vive" (love of life).

Although Bert's done things a bit differently perhaps than most his age, he believes whole-heartedly in the importance of the journey, not just the destination. He's never been one to follow the crowd -- he's an individualist, always has been, always will be. He beats to his own drum and it is perhaps that very beat that has contributed to his heart still beating today.

During his working years, Bert admits he was under a lot of stress like most in their 40s and 50s. But unlike most who just continue under those circumstances while their health suffers, Bert and his wife decided that life was too short. So they forfeited the security of his retirement pension, sold their lake-front home and built a 53-foot ketch to live out their dream by sailing 19K miles around the South Pacific in 3

1/2 years. It was the journey of a lifetime and an extraordinarily healthy experience because when they returned, Bert claimed he was "fighting fit," and vowed good health would be his top priority from that moment forward.

Today, Bert is indeed a walking, talking example of that promise, and it's one he shares gladly with others. His healthy lifestyle became a daily regimen for Bert who continued to eat well and exercise regularly, which included playing tennis almost daily. Bert was so fit that he often scissor jumped over the net after matches and an observer once suggested he consider taking up hurdling with the ease he had jumping over the net.

Bert says he fell in love with hurdling on his very first try. "It's like a feeling of flying," he said. "And it keeps me focused on the importance of stretching, exercising, and eating right so I can keep doing what I love to do -- and keep encouraging others to be healthy too!"

As a world-record hurdler, Bert owns countless records, medals, and championship titles for his track and field accomplishments, and is actually being touted as a legend in the sport. Yet he'll be the first to tell you that it's not about winning, but rather it's the challenge and camaraderie of competition that really keeps him going. But it's also his unique health regimen and passion for life that has really made this man a champ!

Although he ruptured four discs in his back in his early 40s, he never let them operate and instead chose the unconventional route of inverting: hanging upside down, coming up to touch his toes 50 times every morning to strengthen the stomach muscles to better support his back. It's been his routine for over 40 years and as a result, Bert has never had a back problem since. In fact, he claims he's actually healthier now than he ever was in his 40s or 50s, and is living proof that health can actually improve with age.

There's no denying the fact that with age comes increased health risks, and even though Bert was in great shape, he did face a bit of a scare five days after his 89th birthday. "I felt a bit funny that morning, and since it's unusual for me not to feel great everyday when I get up, so I thought I'd better get a second opinion," Bert said.

That was another good call by Bert because by the time he arrived at the hospital, he had a pulse rate of 30 -- which is practically walking dead! Fortunately, all he needed was a pacemaker to keep his heart beating regularly. The doctors were absolutely amazed by his pre-surgery condition and after showing them the pictures of him hurdling, all agreed that hurdling just may have saved his life. He was released the day after surgery, with strict orders to lay low for the next few weeks: no hurdling and no hanging upside down!

"One has to be in pretty good shape to hurdle," said cardiologist Dr. Evans. "Let alone, as an octogenarian. It's pretty remarkable to see that not only did Mr. Morrow survive this episode, he's had virtually no side effects and is expected to make a full recovery to be back at his regular training routine in just a few weeks."

Although Bert's healthy living and eating routine contributed greatly to his remarkable recovery, there's also a powerful inner message that played an equally important role.

"I'm a fighter -- always have been and suspect I always will be," Bert said. "I could have died numerous times before now but I guess I still have work to do here and fortunately I'm still passionate about hurdling, life, and living each day to the fullest so that's what I'm going to continue to do!"

Jim Nichols, 71

&

Mr. Holland's Opus

He's been referred to as 'Mr. Holland's Opus', for his ability to help change children's lives with music. Jim Nichol, 71, recipient of numerous awards for some extraordinary work as a band, music and choir director. But it's certainly not the awards that keep him going, it's his passion for helping kids be proud of themselves and seeing the accomplishments they make as a result.

Nichols spent 29 years as a high school band director, but after only one week of retirement in 1988, he already missed being with kids, so he immediately made himself as a substitute teacher. After a two-year stint, he made another attempt at retirement. And figured that maybe if he moved physically to a new place, he would perhaps recognize that he really was actually "retired."

But even then it was difficult for Nichols to stay away from his passion of music and kids so he signed up to help a local school in his new town. Yet after only a year and a half, Nichols and his wife, Eileen (also a music teacher), were so homesick they returned to their former home town and literally picked up where they left off - continuing to change lives with music.

Nichols immediately found a new school to help with more than 2,000 kids without any music education classes, band, or choir opportunities.

Nichols knew he could help, and to see him in action really is like magic. He can take a student who has never had any exposure to playing a musical instrument, or even any interest in learning about music, and turn them into a musician and lover of music.

When Nichols began this new music program, there were only six students enrolled. By the third week, more than 45 kids had signed up. Today, there are 95 members who proudly march in the band, play their instruments and wear their uniforms, which has resulted in 10 first place competition trophies over the last two and a half years.

"Being so close to the Mexico border, these children never had the opportunity to experience music education before," said a faculty member. "But when given the chance, they were certainly interested. And now, it's become a rather esteemed group to be part of."

Another faculty member remembers when Nichols first started teaching and was assigned to the cafeteria because there weren't any rooms available.

"The faculty lunch area was nearby, so we could hear the group when they first started out," she said. "If you remember the movie, 'Mr. Holland's Opus,' it was literally just like that. The students didn't have a clue how to play or read music, and the sounds that permeated those walls were a far cry from music. But after awhile, it was really exciting to hear them begin playing in tune. From that point forward, what's happened is short of a miracle."

While the task was the "biggest challenge of my life," Nichols was excited about the potential and possibilities. Of course, Nichols had worked his magic before. For example, his first teaching job was at a small school outside Chicago, a farming town where once again, the kids had virtually no previous exposure to music education.

It's really very simple," Nichols said. "I wanted to help kids be proud of themselves -- to make a difference in their lives. Once they feel proud of themselves, then they start to like school, want to come to school and life becomes a new ballgame for them.

Whatever it is, it's definitely working because before the students started in Nichols' music classes, one fourth of them were averaging D and F grades. Now they all carry C averages. Nichols believes it's because they have something to look forward to, something they are part of.

"Music is a team sport," Nichols said. "If you're not doing your part, it's not like someone else can just pick up your instrument and play it too. So the students know others are counting on them and that playing together is the only way they can make the music happen. Music also teaches them how to get along, and helps them recognize how important it is to work together. Those are life lessons that begin with music."

Nichols learned how to play the piano in first grade and by seventh grade he already had his own band. Today, he plays more than 31 different instruments and hasn't missed a single day of work in more than 18 years.

Yes, Nichols has played professionally and held a number of prestigious music related positions over the years. But from the time he held his first teaching position, he immediately knew this was what he was here to do.

"Music is my passion, but teaching music to children is definitely my life's work," Nichols said. "To think that not one of these kids in band takes private lessons and that none of them had ever even held an instrument before, it's tremendously gratifying to see what they have become."

Nichols and his wife of 42 years, Eileen, have also started a scholarship fund to help fund students' future schooling.

"That's what I mean about changing lives," Nichols proudly stated. "We've never left our passion for music, we've just tried to share it with others and the results have certainly made a difference in our lives -- and I think their lives as well."

Red Hat Society

&

Celebrate Life

T he saying, "When I am an old woman I shall wear purple, with a red hat that doesn't go and doesn't suit me..." has often been associated with a new style of aging. But it's actually part of a poem written by Jenny Joseph in 1961, titled "Warning," which has now become the mantra for a delightfully fun women's 50+ age group called "The Red Hat Society," who celebrate life.

"We're like a rebuttal to the 'Empty Nest Syndrome'," Suni Jordan, queen mother of the "Sassy Red Hatters" chapter said with a laugh as she described the organization. "We've done our nurturing, raised our kids and all that, and now it's our turn to nurture ourselves a bit!"

Long before the "Ya Ya Sisterhood," craze, enthusiasm generated by the Red Hat Society began as a result of a few women who decided to greet middle age with verve, humor and élan. The founder, Sue Ellen Cooper, while visiting a friend in Tucson several years ago, impulsively bought a bright red fedora at a thrift shop, for no other reason than it was cheap and she thought, quite dashing. A year or two later she read the poem, "Warning" and decided she'd give a copy of it along with a vintage red hat as birthday gifts to all her friends. Before long, these recipients, so delighted with their gift, started repeating the gift giving among their friends and suddenly this group became the Red Hat Society -- now 150,000 strong in 5,500 chapters worldwide!

"It's all about celebrating life and having fun," said Suni (pronounced like the weather). "And we never let age get in the way of that!"

Unlike many women's organizations, this one is not about charitable fundraising. But that's not to say that these women are not involved with those types of efforts, because many of them are, just not in conjunction with the Red Hat Society.

"This is a group that's just for us," Suni said. "To nurture ourselves and each other by simply being together, playing, enjoying each other's company. We don't ever think about the age thing," Suni shared. "We're enjoying life together with no expectations of each other, other than just accepting each other for who we are."

With a group made up of age 50+ women, many members are widowed or divorced, but regardless of marital and/or life status, the Red Hat Society enables the outrageous side of them to come out.

"Imagine the response to a group of 20+ ladies, all dressed in purple, wearing chic red hats and converging on a local restaurant for lunch," Suni said. "It's quite a site and a way for us to say to the world, 'Hey, look at us -- we're over 50 and we're having a blast! Life is to be lived and celebrated, and we're having fun doing so.'"

You go girls!

Mary Rhea, 75

&

Working in Retirement

Vitality doesn't come in a bottle, and you can't just go pick some up at the store or doctor's office, but rather it's something that starts within ourselves, which seems to grow and flourish as we involve ourselves in projects and/or activities we are passionate about.

Vitality can come from many different forms -- whether it's working on a stimulating project or working out in a stimulating way, but the common link always comes back to being involved in something that fuels us with a type of energy to overcome just about any challenges or opposition that may arise.

As an AARP retirement specialist, I've conducted a number of pre-retirement and retirement programs over the years and one thing that always seems to surprise people is when I tell them they'll likely end up going back to work in some capacity or another. It does seem strange to discuss this possibility while giving a seminar about the transition from work to retirement, however, what is also important to address is the reality of people recognizing that in order to feel fulfilled, one's retirement life is likely going to have to be about more than just rounds of golf and hanging out in the hammock.

With people living longer and healthier than ever before, it's likely we'll spend as much as one third of our life in retirement. That's a long time for a lot of people, and it's far too long to be without any formal structure. So it's not unusual for people to feel they need to fill this time with something fulfilling, to balance some of this free time.

Work can mean different things to different people and it means a completely different thing when we're doing something we want to do versus something we have to do because it's our "job."

There are also a number of different reasons why people work. Some work for economic reasons, some like the sense of accomplishment and there are others who actually enjoy what they do and like the feeling of contributing in whatever way that may be. But again, this is just another example of how work becomes a personal thing with each individual, and just like vitality -- different things drive different people in different ways!

Recently I was contacted as a resource to help identify an "outstanding older worker" to be considered as a nominee for a national award that highlights the valuable contributions older workers are making in their communities and places of work. While there are many, many people to consider for such a prestigious honor, and as many different things they are doing, they all have at least one thing in common: it's not about what it does for them, it's always about doing for others.

Mary Rhea, 75, has always been a planner. Each of her four children was born four years apart -- and it didn't just happen, it was all part of the plan. She was a preacher's wife and the plan was to be a stay-at-home Mom, raise the children, and be available to help out at the church. But once the children were raised and in high school, Rhea was interested in doing some additional planning. This time, however, it involved going to work and becoming a real financial planner.

As one of the first 100 women to become a certified financial planner (CFP) in the United States, Rhea believes she's been put on this earth to help others. This belief, and her work, has become the passion that drives her and as a result, creates a vitality that motivates others, too.

Rhea manages Financial Network Investment where she counsels 300+ clients on money matters and works an average of 50+ hours a week! She admits she's never really thought about retirement and says it was never something she looked forward to -- and to this day, still doesn't.

"It doesn't feel like work because it's so satisfying doing something that helps other people," Rhea said. "I tried retirement, I really did -- for about four months when we moved to Sequim, Washington to retire. But it just didn't cut the mustard for me so here I am back at it with a husband who fortunately understands my mission and supports me all the way."

There are benefits to continuing work, for example Rhea believes being challenged daily is good for the mind and soul -- and the satisfaction of feeling she's contributing some-thing everyday, by helping others, also makes her forget about age.

"Age will never be an issue with me because when you do what you love and feel fulfilled everyday, you don't worry about your age," Rhea said. "Of course I don't know if I ever really thought about whether I'd actually be working at this age -- but I so enjoy it, so why stop now just because of my age?"

It's more than just about money for Rhea, too. She's also involved in Child Help, an organization that supports homes for abused children, and is actively involved with her church, also. She keeps her life balanced by trying to eat right, exercise regularly, and for fun, she and her husband thoroughly enjoy attending local theater productions.

In Rhea's line of work she's obviously seen what it takes to retire happily. She's also all too familiar with one of the critical mistakes people can make -- and it doesn't have anything to do with money.

"If people don't have challenges or hobbies, trips, future goals, whatever, then you're in trouble, regardless of age," Rhea said. "You've got to keep life fresh with new activities, exploring, experiencing new adventures and feeling useful -- that's what keeps you vital and ageless. When you have something in your life that's important and fulfilling, that's what gets you up in the morning and provides the motivation to continue taking care of yourself because you've still got things to do, people to see, and places to go!"

Rosanne Shensa, 88

∞

Qi Gong to Stay Strong

T ake your time, the slower the better," Rosanne Shensa
said as she instructed her students in the bi-weekly
exercise class she's taught for over a decade.

It's an instruction not typically heard at an exercise
class. But this is not your typical class, and certainly not your
typical instructor. Yet the results are certainly one for the
ages.

Rosanne Shensa, who just celebrated her 88th birthday,
thoroughly believes the secret to her longevity and vitality is
her practice of qi gong (pronounced "chee-gong"), which she
offers to others too.

There's obviously something to this gentle form of
exercise that has been recognized in China for over 4,000
years and is embraced by an estimated one hundred million
people who go to parks in the early dawn hours to practice
this physical, mental, and spiritual fitness routine known as qi
gong.

Shensa has established quite an impressive following
herself. Her students range in age from the late 30s to the
early 90s, and travel from all over the county to attend her
classes.

"I'd never had a student older than me before Ruth, 90, who joined about three years ago," Shensa shared. "But we have men, women, couples, a variety of people -- all with different reasons for coming. But one thing they all have in common is the desire to be healthy and to feel good, and that's something everyone can relate to."

Shensa is certainly the reason behind her students' loyalty. Serving as part inspiration, part mentor, Shensa's ability to guide the class through a range of movements which result in improved health is the reason many have been with her for many, many years.

Eileen first came after being diagnosed with breast cancer, understanding that qi gong would help her immune system. She claims it was the reason she survived chemotherapy, a mastectomy, and radiation without every getting sick or missing a class.

Jeanette, one of the younger members, was interested in helping with stress relief. Tony wanted help in mobility, balance and healing energy after his stroke and Delores, diagnosed with lung cancer, was hoping to do something healthy to counter-attack her condition and said the exercise is not only beneficial, but relaxing as well.

In its formal sense, qi gong combines movements, meditation, and breath regulation to enhance the flow of vital energy (called qi) in the body to improve blood circulation and enhance immune functions. Gong means "practice" or "cultivation". So in simple form, qi gong is the cultivation of vital energy.

Vital energy is certainly an appropriate way to describe Shensa. Her flexibility is amazing and she radiates an inner peace that is definitely contagious. She's a long-time student of qi gong and even spent time in China learning the art. The fact that she's survived two heart attacks and a broken hip, while also dealing with osteoporosis, scoliosis and congestive heart failure is impressive enough, but the fact that you'd never know she has any of these conditions is a tribute to her vitality, which she credits to qi gong.

Qi gong is believed to do a number of wonderful things which is undoubtedly the reason for its growing, almost cult following now in western civilization. From preventing

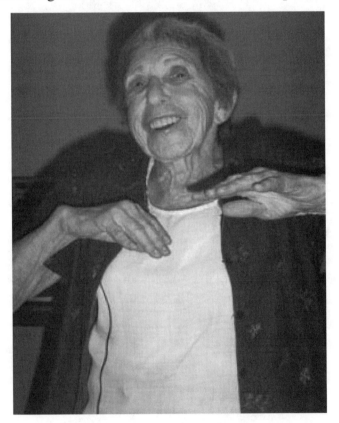

illness to stopping the progression of disease, strengthening and detoxifying vital organs, strengthening bones, muscles, ligaments and tendons, relieving stress, increasing mental clarity, promoting tranquility and vibrancy and greatly slowing, and even reversing our body's aging process certainly helps explain why so many give it a try.

Caleb Elroy Shikles, 91

&

Life Lessons

It was only 9:00 AM when I made my first call to Caleb Elroy Shikles, 91, but he was already out and about beginning his day. Tuesdays are his "school days" and there are a number of life lessons people of all ages could learn from spending some time with Caleb.

He considers himself an "adventurer of life" and although Caleb never expected to live this long, he firmly believes life is a gift. If we're going to be here occupying space, we need to be accountable by continuing to make a positive difference.

Caleb has spent a lifetime making a positive difference. He served 68 years as an American Baptist Minister and describes his aging as a form of ministry in itself. "I'm in the adolescence of old age," Caleb said. "I really don't feel old within myself, and while some may marvel at how I live, I think fewer people would be afraid of growing older if they'd worry less about how old they are and focus more on continuing to live life every day."

Caleb's life is full, and so are his days. On the day we met, I was lucky to be squeezed in during the one hour he took for lunch. His morning started early with the Men's Breakfast Club, followed by his 10:00 AM singing class and his 11:00 AM writing class. After lunch, he was off to his

1:00 PM Brain Aerobics class, taught by a Ph.D. who works with the students on memory and mind exercises, followed by his 4:00 PM Current Events class taught by a lawyer. "Classes and learning are stimulating," Caleb explained. "We aren't here in this life to just vegetate, we're here to touch people purposely."

While Caleb continues to enjoy life's adventures (he just recently returned from a group trip to Rome in which all of his nine fellow travelers were women), he also spends a lot of time helping others. From his "Rolling Readers" tutoring at a local elementary school to his "Listening Post" for residents and staff, and even a special program for those with Alzheimers, Caleb believes it's people's responsibility to give back.

It's evident Caleb continues to connect with people. He's a gregarious soul who always has a smile on his face as he swiftly walks the halls, going here and there, greeting everyone along the way by name. As a six-year resident of a retirement community, Caleb thoroughly enjoys the array of people and activities available to him.

"People my age need to learn they need to do more helping!" Caleb said. "I guess some think that because we've lived so long we deserve to just sit back, relax, and do nothing. None of us "deserve" anything in this life. It's never been about what you get - it's what you give that truly counts."

Certainly Caleb is making every minute of his life count, and he lives his life by the golden rule: It's not about whether your life was successful; it's about whether your life was significant.

That's indeed a life lesson for the ages -- and all ages.

Carol Sing, 58

ॐ

Oldest Woman To Swim the English Channel

W hat is it about some people who are able to overcome all odds and accomplish things few of us
could ever imagine doing, let alone actually doing?
I've always been intrigued by what makes these people tick,
and am continually amazed to discover that in general, we all
have what it takes -- it's within each one of us. The difference
may only be in the trying and applying.

It's always inspiring to hear that at some point along
the way, even these amazing achievers, uttered the word
'never' prior to their accomplishment. But they're also quick
learners and recognize that it's dangerous to say 'never'
because inevitably, that changes.

One such person who I met recently is Carol Sing, 58,
a long-distance swimmer who became the oldest woman ever
to navigate the English Channel. Three years ago, while
accompanying her swimming partner Bob to England for his
successful attempt at this feat, Carol remembers telling herself
she would never do that. But she did, and just look at her
now.

Carol's about as real and down-to-earth as any human
can be. She's amazed by all the fanfare her swim has created
because she wasn't after any recognition. She was just out to
have a good time, with a good swim, on a good day, and
August 20, 1999 had it all!

"I really believe this was just meant to be," Carol claimed. "Of course it does take a fair amount of training and sticking with a schedule. But the elements were exceptional that day. It was sunny, which is amazing in itself for England, the water wasn't too cold at 63 degrees, the swells and the current were tolerable, so I was able to complete my mission in 12 hours and 32 minutes. I started at 6 a.m. in England, the day before my 58th birthday, and finished the 21.5 mile swim to France at 6:32 p.m."

Make no mistake; Carol has been athletically inclined all her life. She swims daily, was the swim coach at a local high school, but admits she never dreamed she'd be doing this.

"The last time I was in England, was to support Bob's attempt at the Channel. And although I swore I would 'never' swim that, it did inspire me to train for the 21-mile Catalina Channel," Carol remembered. "Although petrified on my first attempt, I made it, which inspired me to challenge myself one step further and train for the 28-mile swim around Manhattan Island in New York which I did last year! All of these steps and attempts got me here. But there was never any set mission, it just all eventually led to this."

Perhaps the secret's in the actual doing and not giving yourself the chance to change your mind or time to concentrate on all the reasons why you shouldn't or can't. Just continue going forward towards new goals and accomplishments and eventually you most likely will achieve.

As I watched and listened to Carol display and describe what she did that now-famous August 20th day (a day when five others also made the English Channel attempt, yet only three others were successful, another was forced to quit and one even died from hypothermia) it became very apparent that what it takes to achieve things like this comes from deep-down within. No fancy, high-tech gear or nutritional supplements for this dame, just "my regular one-piece swimsuit, my neon green bubble-swim cap, a little 'grease' (nothing more than lanolin and Vaseline on the body to prevent chafing), my ear-plugs, and goggles, and I'm good to go!"

But what you can't buy in any store or find on any shelf is what Carol and many others who accomplish amazing feats have in abundance -- the psychological edge. She states that this experience was as much psychological as it was physical, and believes her ability to stay relaxed and focused mentally, is likely what got her through.

"I was so seasick the first six hours," Carol remembered. "But I just persevered and knew I'd eventually be able to work through it. That's the key really, to believe it will get better and to get your mind out of thinking anything different. Fifty-percent was mental. When I got in that water I said 'this Channel is mine!' and I meant it. You really have to become one with the elements. Through visualization you become part of the water and enter a meditative state through the rhythm you create with your own breathing and movement with each stroke. In many ways, you trick your mind into thinking about other things. It's peaceful that way and I really enjoy it!"

An inspiring story that reminds us life is in the trying -- and that is in our control!

Jack Sogorka

ॐ

A Healthy Healing Attitude

Jack Sogorka, 78, has always been good with his hands, and fixing things is one of his favorite activities -- it just really makes him tick. Yet imagine the challenge he faced when he broke both his hands from a slip on his hillside while trimming a tree. And imagine the frustration he faced daily with "the shakes" or "tremors" he experienced in both his arms and hands for over 25 years. But Jack never let it get him down, he continued to persevere and the results are amazing -- maybe even a medical miracle.

Jack has battled high blood pressure for most of his adult life. "For thirty or forty years my blood pressure was routinely 200+ over 108 or so," Jack shared. "I'm diabetic, I had angina, but ever since I had that stroke in March -- I've never been better! The shakes are gone, my blood pressure is down to 136 over 68, I'm off the insulin and glycerin tablets and now my sugar levels are routinely reading under 100 -- down from over 350 or more!"

Perhaps not a medical miracle, but it is an amazing story. Much of Jack's health improvements can undoubtedly be attributed to a combination of the right medication, which enabled his body to endure the unclogging of a 98% carotid artery -- and the stroke that occurred during the surgery. Glucophage is the medication Jack describes as the miracle treatment, but doctors have no idea how the stroke stopped the shakes.

"The doctors could never really explain why I had the tremors to begin with, other than being a result perhaps of my high blood pressure, carotid artery, and diabetes," Jack said. "But when I woke up after the surgery even though I was unable to talk without slurred speech, or write my name, I had no signs of the shakes and that was truly unbelievable!"

While most might worry about not being able to talk or work their hands properly after suffering a stroke, Jack remained optimistic because he'd been through therapy before.

"When I broke both my hands, I had to do an extensive amount of physical therapy, and that experience taught me that if you stay with it, be patient, and continue to work hard -- good things would happen," Jack shared. "I believed that, and still do, so I consider myself a lucky, happy man."

Jack admits he never really was scared. Even after discovering his limited abilities from the stroke, Jack believes he was so excited about the good that came, perhaps he subconsciously chose to focus on the positive changes rather than just the negative.

"I was in the hospital three weeks for recovery, working with speech and physical therapists daily, sometimes several times a day," Jack shared. "And during that time I noticed how negative patients were, which you certainly can understand when one's trying to recover and you don't feel well. But I really do think that attitude can either help or hinder us. Whether you're recovering in a hospital or dealing with regular life challenges -- what and how we think definitely affects us."

Jack shared one example in particular, the food -- which everyone always seems to have an opinion about, and generally not a positive one when you're referring to hospital servings. While all the patients around him complained about "the mush" they were being served, Jack's opinion of the oatmeal was terrific. In fact, he always hoped for seconds!

Now maybe that really doesn't have anything to do with the food and instead is just the way Jack is. He admits he is a relatively positive person and even when the chips are down, he chooses to look at the bright side. But when there's so much in medicine we don't understand, is it possible that this way of thinking may actually affect our healing?

The nurses and therapists apparently enjoyed his sunny disposition, because the day he was discharged, they awarded him a diploma for being a prize patient and for all his positive efforts and accomplishments.

"It's not my style to give in or give up on anything, whether it's my own health or a challenging work project. I'd get more frustrated if I didn't persevere and gave up trying," Jack said. "Healing and life require the same perseverance. You can't just sit back, complain and give up by succumbing. You've got to go at it and attack it positively."

Jack's doctors and nurses are certainly thrilled with his current health status, but they do miss him. You see, Jack used to go to the doctor once or twice a week, but now it's only once or twice every two or three months! No one knows for sure what it's all attributed to, but it seems to be more than just the result of his new medication and successful surgery -- the mindset and attitude has undoubtedly made a significant contribution, too.

"I'll tell you what, it's like starting a whole new life!" Jack exuberantly said. "I feel better honestly, than I have in forty years."

Of course, Jack continues to challenge himself with

projects he enjoys -- he's still good with his hands and at fixing things. But perhaps more than anything, Jack says these are happy days and he looks forward to each new dawn. He chooses to look at what he has, rather than what he's lost, and that's a healthy, healing attitude indeed.

Super Senior Surfers

&

Never Too Old To Be Stoked

S urfing is one of those ageless activities -- people of all ages can do it and do. So if you think surfing's just for the young, then you haven't checked out the legendary long boarders at just about any special surfing spot.

I recently met a group of fun-loving, self-described "watermen" who have been surfing longer than some of us have been alive. With ages ranging from 64 to 88, most all of them have surfed for well over 50 years -- starting out in the late 1930s.

"We surfed year-round with the unforgiving, old-time plank boards," said Bud Caldwell, 79. "No leashes, no wet-suits, and boards that weighed between 75 to 100 pounds."

Surfing was certainly considered a workout in those days. Just getting those boards to the water, paddling out, catching a few waves, and then lugging that now wet and even heavier board back up the beach would be more than many surfers today could even begin to handle.

But time's change and technology is such that today's long boards weigh in around 20 pounds on average -- making surfing a much more popular and do-able sport for the masses.

Yet while some aspects of this beloved sport have changed, many things have stayed the same, which undoubtedly is one of the reasons for surfing's ever-growing popularity. The camaraderie, friendships, being outdoors and one with nature, while enjoying the health benefits of regular exercise and doing something fun that you love to do, are among the many reasons why these grandfathers and great-grandfathers all say they still surf.

"Hadj" formally known as William Hein, 85, rode his first wave here in 1938. Despite his heart bypass surgery, Hadj is still at it today -- surfing five days a week on a 9'8 Hanky Warner designed long board, and claims the friendships and keeping himself in shape is why he's still at it.

At 88, Dan O'Connell (who Hadj recently nicknamed "Piano Man" since there are 88 keys on a piano), is the senior member of the team and although his last board ride was at age 86, Dan still swims daily, paddles out with the guys and recognizes the benefits of being in the water and continuing to move around.

As one of the youngsters, Billy "Goldy" Goldsmith, 79, believes surfing has kept him alive. "It's given me a will to live and the positive spirit through the camaraderie has been the best part," he said. Busy working and raising a family, "Goldy," as his friends call him, quit for about 20 years until his 50s when his children started surfing and wanted him to join them. Thirty years later he's still at it and enjoying every moment of it.

For Les Bartlet, 68 "and a half," he says with a smile, and Ron St. John, 64, they say just being around these guys is an inspiration in itself. "They're the common thread, the history, and a great group of guys," said St. John. "Age just isn't an issue when you're surfing -- and they're proving it."

As the gang turned and walked away, headed for breakfast together at a local diner, on the back of "Goldy's" T-Shirt read a saying that captured it all, "Old Guys Rule!"

"If we've gotta age, we've gotta dig it!" said one of the bunch.

Never too old to be stoked, it's obvious that continuing to do what you love to do is one of the secrets to growing older in a healthy, happy way.

Women s Hoops

&

Doing Something For The First Time

W hen was the last time you did something for the first time? One of the "secrets" to happy, healthy aging is continuing to learn, explore, and try new things. Yet one of the other most important aspects is to never let your age deter you from a new experience, activity, or adventure. Those who do, often feel "old" before their time -- yet those who don't are often forever young at heart.

I recently met up with an interesting group of ladies playing hoops, who never in their wildest dreams imagined they'd be doing this at this stage in their lives. But that's what makes life interesting and exciting -- trying new things, particularly at a time when you least expect it

"I walked by the courts one Sunday afternoon and did a double take. I couldn't believe what I was seeing," remembered Connie Leigh, 62. "They certainly weren't your typical looking basketball jocks, more like typical looking Grandmas who were zipping down the courts, whooping it up, giving high-fives and obviously having a heck-of-a lot of fun!"

Connie stood and watched in awe and amazement for several minutes before one of the players approached her and said, "Honey, would you like to shoot some hoops with us? I don't think you're old enough to play on our team, but come on out here and dribble on down the court with us if you'd like!"

That was more than three years ago and the fun hasn't stopped since for Connie. Although she was too young to play on that initial team (they were a 70+ team who had won the Gold Medal in the National Senior Olympics), Connie was immediately recruited to a team in her age group and has since experienced more enjoyment, fanfare, camaraderie, and good health than she ever could have imagined.

"I didn't have a clue about anything. I had virtually no training," Connie laughed. "We didn't have the free clinics then like they offer now. In fact, I can remember being coached on how to guard by one of the gals on the team who took me out on the court with a big plastic trash can and taught me how to guard with that! That can was mine! I was all over it, and that's how I learned."

Today the practices are a bit more sophisticated and no experience is necessary. It doesn't matter whether you've played before or not. All you need is the dream to be part of a team and you're good to go.

"I was happy to learn that we were only playing half-court and not having to run up and down the full court," Connie said. "And actually, even though I'm older than I was when I started, I'm definitely in much better shape! I remember only being able to play about three minutes before I was gasping for breath. Now I can go two hours and feel simply great!"

This is a diverse group of women who genuinely enjoy not only the opportunity they now have to play, but also the camaraderie they share.

"We are schoolteachers, homemakers, bankers, real estate agents, retirees, business professionals, grandmothers, great-grandmothers, you name it -- we've got it!" Connie said. "We're having a ball, literally. And we want other women to know they can too! Too many people think you have to give up on these ideas and types of activities as you get older, but this has put fun back in our lives and ultimately, this probably helps us from feeling 'old'. There weren't a lot of women sports opportunities when we were younger, so we're enjoying this and there's no way age is going to stop us now."

SUPER SENIORS
THE BEST OF VOLUME I

෪

Banana George Blair, 83

&

Barefoot Water Skiier

T he doctor's exact words were, "You'll probably never
water-ski again, George, and certainly never barefoot.
You're too old to recover from an injury like this."
But those words also inspired the drive that makes "Banana"
George Blair so unique. He's a legend, an inspiration, and is
considered the international ambassador of water-skiing and
barefooting.

George skis fast, often, and thinks it's a heck of a lot of
fun. He was the first person to water-ski on all seven conti-
nents, which earned him a place in The Guinness Book of
World Records at the age of 74. He was inducted into the
American Water Ski Hall of Fame at the age of 76, and was
the barefoot-jumping record holder from age 69 to 76. Today
he still performs, just as he has for thirty-plus years, in the ski
show at Cypress Gardens, the oldest and longest-running
entertainment show in the world -- and the grandest water-skiing display ever.

"Barefooting is a contact sport, so there is the risk of
injury, particularly when you're going 35-40 MPH and crash
against the water," said George, describing his trade.
"Barefooting is extreme, but I'm the king of hard hits," he
claimed. "I've had a few nasty falls that have resulted in
injuries, but nothing will stop my 'just do it' attitude, including
a doctor who says I can't. 'Can't' just doesn't exist in my
world."

George took up the sport of water-skiing at age 40 and although his first experience with barefooting came at age 46, he really didn't start competing until he was 64. Since then he's become an inspiration to people of all ages.

"It's amazing to see all the mail I get, and I always get a kick out of the young kids who tell me they just hope they'll still be able to walk when they get to be my age! And to those who say I'm too old to be doing this, I tell them they're the ones missing out on all the fun!"

But George is not just about water-skiing. He's also a self-made millionaire, businessman, philanthropist, art connoisseur, actor, photographer, world traveler and musician -- all as an octogenarian. His zest and zeal for life and his "no barrier" lifestyle will likely continue to make George one of life's most interesting characters.

Recently clad in his bright yellow wetsuit, yellow sunglasses, sandals, and toting a banana-yellow long board, George just took up surfing, too! It was on his 'to do' list as an activity he'd always been curious about, so why not give it a try? That's just part of his style. Amazingly, but typical of George's athleticism and water-sport agility, he even stood up on his very first try. "I love to feel the wind in my face and the energy rush through my body by trying new things. I learned how to snowboard at the age of 75, surf at 83, and my latest kick is racecar driving because I do love to go fast!"

Proving you're never too old to try something new, George joined the Skip Barber Racing School and fulfilled a longtime dream of racecar driving. "Driving the racecar also proved to me that my mind and body still work as well as they did when I was 70, or 22 for that matter. So what's age got to do with it?" George asked. "It's the fun, experience, and exhilaration of a new challenge that makes life interesting to me. And if it involves going fast, sign me up!"

To say George has left an impression on this earth is an understatement. And if you were wondering where the nickname "Banana" George comes from, it's not just his bright yellow wetsuit, cars, phones, houses, and boats -- he gives away more than three tons of Chiquita bananas every year too! George believes they are quite possibly nature's most perfect food because they are loaded with vitamins, minerals, and water, and have lots of energy-enhancing qualities.

So if it's energy you're after, take it from George "Stay curious, be active, have fun eat bananas, and make the most of each and every day!"

In Memory Of
Jeanne Calment, 122
℘

Oldest Person in the World

S he holds a place in history as the oldest person in the world. Jeanne Calment was born February 21, 1875 and died August 4, 1997, at the age of 122. She lived a good life, and indeed a long life -- a life in which she was "never bored," in her words. Jeanne experienced the invention of the telephone and radio, was fourteen when the Eiffel Tower was completed in 1889, and even remembered meeting Vincent Van Gogh.

Yet how she experienced her later years was as extraordinary as the life she lived. She took up the sport of fencing at 85 and still rode her bike at the age of 100. She powdered her cheeks with a dab of red rouge and only quit smoking and having her daily glass of wine at the age of 117. Though blind and nearly deaf at the time of her death, Jeanne remained spirited and mentally sharp all the way to the end.

Unaware that she would live so long, Jeanne sold her apartment when she was 90 to a local lawyer, on an annuity system under which he would inherit it after she died. But after paying out for thirty years, the lawyer died at age 77 without ever taking possession of her home. Jeanne outlived her husband, brother, daughter, and even her grandson; she left no direct descendants.

Her birthday parties were like national events, with well-wishers from all over the world wanting to know her secrets to living such a long life. Always gracious, many fondly remember how Jeanne showed her appreciation. On her 100th birthday, she rode her bicycle all over town and thanked those who helped her celebrate!

Jeanne Calment will always be remembered as a true model of hope and inspiration to all.

Mary Cunningham, 90

&

90th Birthday Skydive

When you make plans for innovative birthday celebrations, by the time you reach the age of 90 the ideas seem to get more and more unique. "The sky's the limit" became the theme for Mary's day, which actually included a tandem skydive from 15,000 feet!

"I've done just about everything else, so why not a parachute jump from a plane for my birthday?" Mary laughed. "Oh, it was such a thrill. I loved every minute of it!"

Mary obviously has no fear of heights, since she's taken to the sky for other birthday celebrations, too, all in various parts of California. She rode a glider over the mountains in Hemet for her 70th, spent her 75th in a hot-air balloon over the Temecula Valley, and her 80th was a fun-filled day of roller-coasters at Magic Mountain.

"I thought a new birthday adventure was in order every five years, but now I think we should do it every year, so on my 91st, I'm thinking a white-water raft trip might be fun!" Mary said. "It'll be hard to top this, but I'm willing to give it a try! My friends think I'm a little nuts, but that's O.K. -- somebody's got to do it. Most people know I'm pretty unpredictable and spontaneous, but that's what keeps life interesting, don't you think?"

Not all of her fun comes from the air; her 85th birthday was spent driving through Glacier National Park in Montana. Mary admits she has a bit of the travel bug. She's been in almost all of the fifty states and believes her sense of adventure, continual going, doing, and having fun have definitely been key to her healthy aging.

The plan for her 90th birthday was a toss-up between a bungee jump and the parachute skydive, but while watching the bungee cord's jerking motion as it retracted, Mary liked the gentle floating of the parachute jump better.

"When I told my niece Jeanie, and her husband Larry, that I thought the skydive would be fun, they quickly went to work seeking out the best man for the job. They found him, and although he admitted he'd never filled a request like mine, to his knowledge I am the oldest jumper ever!"

Although she's always been something of a daredevil, both Mary's family and the instructor were adamant that she get a doctor's clearance before she embarked on her latest endeavor. The doctor gave her a clean bill of health, and with a thumbs-up sign of approval he sent her on her way to be fitted for her birthday flight suit.

"I got all gussied up in a brand-new outfit -- a jumpsuit with all the gear I needed for my birthday fun . . . a flight up and a jump down with a soft, safe landing," Mary said. "They coached me with training tips and most importantly how, when, and where to pull the rip cord. They told me to smile, too, but I was afraid I might lose my dentures way up there! I wasn't scared at all though. In fact, I told jokes on the ride up. When I was ready to jump, I remember looking down and being absolutely amazed by all the houses we could see below."

Mary got a little extra special treatment for her jump: instead of taking the plane up to just 12,500 feet, they decided to take her an additional 2,500 feet higher so she could enjoy the view and ride a little longer -- an extra seventy-seconds, to be exact. "It was so peaceful, serene, and beautiful up there . . . you just can't imagine! But I was afraid to smile for fear I might lose my dentures way up there. Mary said. "Then, there must have been two hundred people on the ground ready to greet me -- all smiling and giving me a thumbs-up for a job well done, including a TV news crew."

Mary's family notified the local news stations about the event. They were told that if it was a slow news day, they might send someone out to film it. It was a slow day, so Mary's birthday party was seen not only on the local news but all across the country and internationally as well. "Thank god for a slow news day!" Mary said. "We got calls from friends all over the place. Even my great-grandniece in Holland . . . I became a celebrity overnight! I just ate it up. It's beautiful when something so unexpected happens. It really was a lot of fun!"

For the most part, Mary's life is fun. She keeps herself busy crocheting Afghans, knitting baby clothes, sweaters, and puppet mittens or creating Teddy Roosevelt replica teddy bears for hospital patients. She says she's always doing something, and feels sorry for people who just give up.

"After my stroke at 88, I could have given up, but that's just not my style," Mary said. Mary initially lost her hearing, speech, and had difficulty moving her legs, but daily physical therapy and family support enabled her to regain her strength.

She admits she was never overly health-conscious and recognizes she did some unhealthy things when she was younger, but figures she's made up for it in her later years, and believes it's never too late to do so.

Birthdays will always be fun memories for Mary, who keeps a journal, highlighting some of her fondest memories and special adventures, which she someday hopes to publish for her family.

"I'll do that one of these days -- when I'm old," Mary said. And when asked when that might be and what old was, Mary simply shrugged her shoulders, smiled and said with a twinkle in her eye, "I don't know, I'll let you know when I get there!"

Norton, 79, & Betty Davey, 78

&

Oldest Ironman Triathlete

I magine biking 150 miles, running 30 to 40 miles and swimming 300 laps every week, all for the pure joy of fitness and competition. This is the "retirement" regimen of Norton Davey. And to think it has come to all this after a simple recommendation from his company's medical director to add a little exercise to his life some twenty-four years ago.

Since then, Norton has become a testimony to athleticism at any age and a role model for a new generation of seniors finding that life can begin with retirement. He climbs some of the world's tallest mountains, including the 19,341-foot Mt. Kilimanjaro in Africa, runs marathons, and competes annually with the elite in his age group in one of the most challenging events known to man: the Ironman Triathlon in

Kona, Hawaii. In fact, Norton is one of only two men in the world who have ever completed the Ironman, after the age of 75, and he's competed in the event fifteen times in the past sixteen years!

The Ironman event begins with a 2.4-mile open-ocean swim followed by a 112-mile bike ride, and ends with a 26.2-mile run -- a mere sixteen-hour workout for Norton, all back-to-back and in one day. He does it because he feels great and enjoys the competition.

Although he's unique, Norton says he tries to live his life as an example for others. "I noticed when I first started exercising, which wasn't until I was 60, that just by walking and then running, three things happened. First and foremost, I felt better. Not that I ever really felt bad, but I lost some weight and just felt great. Second, my vital signs improved, which also explains why I felt better, and third, I entered my first 10K race and got "hooked" on competition."

Norton claims it was a slow process -- he didn't just start doing all this overnight. It took time, obviously, to work up to the triathlon level. In fact he remembers when he first started swimming he could barely make the length of the pool, and as for running, he could barely get around the block walking.

Most of us have heard about the health benefits of exercise, particularly with age, but few have the stamina to take on a feat like Norton's. However, that too may be changing because there s definitely more company in his age group than ever before. When he competed in his first Ironman at the age of 63, there were only four others over the age of 60. Since then he has been the oldest finisher in at least six Ironman events. In the 1997 event there were four others joining him in the 75-and-over age bracket, and more than fifty-five participants over the age of 60.

"The secret to aging is definitely out," Norton said. "To stay healthy, stay active, and to stay active, stay healthy! I believe our bodies are capable of more than we give them credit for, particularly as we get older. And if you commit to a safe, sensible exercise routine and good healthy diet -- who knows how long we might be able to go!"

Norton has not done this all alone, however. He gives a lot of credit to his beautiful bride of fifty-five years, Betty, 78, who has continually supported his efforts. Betty also has maintained an active lifestyle, and after suffering a mild stroke, she realized just how much of a role exercise has played in her health and recovery process.

"I actually started exercising twenty-three years ago, at the age of 55, and have been very consistent in my routine," Betty said. "I've pedaled more than 53,000 miles on my stationary bike, riding thirty minutes a day. I attend a "lite" aerobics class three times a week, followed by a stretch class. I lift light weights -- two to three pound hand weights two or three times a week, and then on my 'off' days of no classes, I walk briskly for about forty-five minutes to an hour, totaling three to four miles."

Betty and her doctors will be the first to admit that it was this exercise routine that they credit not only her speedy recovery, but also the mildness of her stroke. She remembers the doctors -- from her cardiologist and ophthalmologist to her neurologist, all unanimously agreeing that if Betty had not been in such good physical condition, her stroke would have been much worse.

Certainly exercise contributed greatly to her recovery, but Betty also credits years of healthy eating. She has been almost a vegetarian most of her life, serving lots of fruits, vegetables, and salads to her family over the years. And she also recognizes the role that a balanced life and loving family play to her good health and long life, too.

"I am both thankful and fortunate for all the good in my life," Betty said. "Loving parents who never 'put me down' while I was growing up, a loving husband, family, and friends, as well as being a happy person with a good attitude and outlook on life, have all contributed to how I am today. I'm proud of my age. In fact, on my 78th birthday I announced to my exercise class how great I felt. My wish for them was for them to all feel the same when they get to be my age!"

Together, Norton and Betty continue to be a team committed to helping others believe that it's never too late to incorporate healthy activities into one's lifestyle, and to benefit from them. They lead by example and are definitely an inspiration to follow.

Florence Foster, 94

&

Fun-Seeking Entrepreneur

Florence feels that fun and faith are the foundations for her longevity, and at age 94, she also recognizes that being blessed with good health has played a part, too. But the real secret to her aging success may be her spunky, get-up-and-go outlook on life. "I have fun all the time -- age has nothing to do with that!" she said. Not only is she having fun in her own life, she's helping others have fun too.

Florence figured it was time for a change in the design of the ugly gray metal canes used by people in her age group. Her drive for fun and ingenuity launched a fabulous new spin on the old-fashioned cane, changing the product's tired image into one exemplifying creativity, uniqueness, and definite personality.

"I was headed for Arizona to hike with my daughter and knew it would be helpful if I had a little support, like a cane, for the uneven surfaces of the terrain. But my only choice was the standard hospital rental, and that just wouldn't do it for me -- those were for old people!" Florence said. "If I used one of those, people would've started treating me as if I was old . . . and then I might believe them!"

Florence set out to find a way to add a little color and fun to the old cane concept. She found herself at a local auto-parts factory asking for a clear plastic tube about one inch in diameter that could be filled with different things and have a handle and rubber tip applied at the ends. It was "do-able," she was told, and the next thing she knew, presto -- Florence became an entrepreneur! The Florence Foster cane is sold all over the country, so now others can experience the fun and freedom it provides, too.

"The first one I made for myself was filled with a string of colorful mini silk roses, and when I took it to Arizona, I could barely leave the house without someone asking me about my walking stick," Florence remembered. "I know there are a lot of people like me who could use the support of a cane to get around better and more often but would never use one of those other ones. But there really weren't any other options," Florence said. "The cane's image may not be good, but the concept is great . . . it just needed a little updating and some creativity. Now, maybe those who've never used one before will give it a try, have some fun and even get out and do more without the risk and fear of falling."

Since starting this venture, Florence has received letters from people all over the country who are thoroughly enjoying her product and their new lifestyle. "It's not about making money, it's the great stories people send telling me of their newfound freedom and even friendships that have developed since they've used their new canes. One of my favorites was from a granddaughter who bought one for her grandmother's 100th birthday! She had not been very active, but ever since she got her birthday cane she's gone nonstop, showing it off to all her friends and even made new friends in the process."

Florence firmly believes that faith has played a significant role in her life and that God had this very plan in mind for her to "give other older adults some fun -- to get 'em out and get 'em going again," and her Foster cane is now enabling that to happen.

"Life is meant to be celebrated, that's the way I see it," Florence said. "Every morning I read a Bible verse I have taped to my mirror: 'This is the day the Lord has made, Rejoice and be glad in it!' That is how I start and live every day of my life. You just can't have a bad day after that -- rejoicing makes it a good day!"

With the personal motto "If it is meant to be, it is up to me!" Florence is determined to help others and herself have fun in life. She will continue her daily exercises to keep her good health, stay involved with photography, church, family, and friends and continue to live a "balanced" life with a good attitude -- so she can stay healthy and happy and have fun a little while longer.

Rose Freedman, 104

℅

Laker Fanatic

Rose couldn't be happier, the Los Angeles Lakers basketball team is off to their best start ever, 11-0! "It's the best start in the history of the franchise," said Rose, who may know more about the Lakers than most fans half her age.

Rose is indeed a sports fan, but she's an absolute Lakers fanatic! And she just may have something to do with this season's great start since she was sitting with Lakers owner Jerry Buss, on opening night. "They call me their 'Lucky Charm.' I'm definitely one of their biggest fans, and probably one of the oldest, too. That's what keeps me young -- staying involved with all the things I love!"

Being a sports fan has come full circle for Rose. She raised three children, including two boys, and doubts there are many mothers with sons who don't get hooked on sports. Today her entire family, including the grandkids, is into sports -- especially Laker basketball, and matriarch Rose leads the way.

"To say she goes through withdrawal during the off-season is an understatement," said Rose's daughter, Arlene. "The whole family is always happy to see the basketball season begin. At least we always know where Mom will be -- watching her beloved Lakers!"

Evidently the Lakers are equally proud to have a fan like Rose. In honor of her 100th birthday, they paid a special tribute to her at half time with a plaque naming Rose the Lakers number one fan. She also got a happy birthday serenade from the entire team, band, and enthusiastic crowd. "I was out there in the middle of the court celebrating my 100th birthday with the Lakers! Jerry West gave me a Lakers jersey with my name in letters on the back, and number 100 to boot! Plus, A. C. Green, Byron Scott, and James Worthy were with me too. It was unbelievable and unforgettable!"

Her love for the Lakers is genuine and apparently is reciprocated. Whenever she sees any of the players around town, she is always amazed when they remember her and stop to visit. "After Magic left, I told James Worthy he was my favorite, so now he always seems to remember me!" Of course, it's easy to see why Rose is so easy to remember. She has a great outlook on life and is in good health except for being a little hard of hearing. She takes no pills, loves to shop, thrives on learning, and believes family is always number one.

"My family is the most important thing in my life and they are what really keeps me going," Rose proudly shared. "They treat me nice and are always watching over, so I feel truly blessed to have such a loving and caring family."

Rose also takes good care of herself. She still lives on her own, exercises daily, and loves to cook, but has recently started having lunch out and says she's really enjoying this new special treat. "After cooking all these years, even though I love it, it's a nice change of pace to go out for lunch. Maybe I should have done this sooner since I'm having so much fun, but I guess it's better late than never!"

One thing Rose is rarely late for and certainly never misses is a sale! In fact, she readily admits that one of her favorite pastimes is shopping. Rose says you're never too old for a bargain. "She's undoubtedly one of the most elegant women I know," Arlene said. "And she dresses to the nines. The phrase 'California casual' never made its way to her wardrobe. Of course, that's because she was a career woman in New York and always dressed to the hilt -- she knows no different. She's never worn a pair of sweats or jeans in her life and probably never will. Dressing casual to her means a skirt and blouse, with heels and nylons too!"

In fact, on one of her latest trips to Mexico she walked the town's cobblestone streets in heels! Sneakers, though offered and undoubtedly more comfortable, were completely unacceptable to her. She considered them an appalling accessory to her attire -- a fashion statement she was not about to make.

The trip to Mexico was planned to fulfill her continual love of learning, Spanish specifically, because languages are her passion. "My daughter took me to San Miguel de Allende, a famous artist's colony four hours north of Mexico City, which has an institute where foreigners go to learn Spanish. We went to school every day and lived right there in their community in order to experience their culture in a unique and meaningful way. "I speak six different languages and can even read and write many of them too. I just love to learn, always have and expect I always will," Rose shared.

Rose believes you're never too old to learn new things and that learning keeps you young. As a result, she says she never feels old. "I learned about baseball this year, too, by going to my first professional ballgame. How about that, seeing your first Dodgers game at 104?" But if the Dodgers are looking for a good-luck charm, they'd better look again, because another professional sports team in town has already spoken for Rose.

Dr. Margaret Holden Jones, 93

&o

First Time Bride at 85

D r. Margaret Holden Jones has a passion for life. Professionally, she is recognized as a pioneer in the treatment of cerebral palsy. For her extraordinary, sixty-five year career passionately dedicated to improving the lives of both children and adult CP patients in the United States, she received the first Lifetime Achievement Award.

Margaret was one of the first women to graduate from Cornell Medical School in 1933. In the field of CP research, she is credited with recognizing the need to treat infants early with daily therapy. Margaret also initiated the philosophy of comprehensive care for CP treatment, addressing the need to treat all of the patient's symptoms in an attempt to improve their total quality of life.

Today she still hasn't stopped. She continues to serve as an advocate for people with cerebral palsy and thoroughly believes there is still much work to be done. Margaret contributes in her typically devoted way -- every week she hitches a ride to UCLA to volunteer her services at the CP clinic, where physicians seek her out for input on a variety of specialty cases.

Beyond her professional life, there is a vibrant individual who has a true love for and understanding of the real meaning of life. "My desire is to always keep growing -- to stay involved is what life is all about. I've always believed life is what you make it, so we should always make the most of it. That's why my contributions will continue throughout my entire life."

Although time has caught up with Margaret's vision, that doesn't deter her from continuing to keep current in the scientific and medical world where she has played such an essential role. She utilizes a large-screen television and two automated reading machines, including one that views documents and even reads them back to her.

One of the most beautiful things in Margaret's life occurred at the age of 85, when she entered into her first (and only) marriage, to Dr. Adrian C. Kanaar. "I was never really looking to fall in love, but I also hadn't given up on the possibility either. I hoped I would meet 'Mr. Right' someday -- it just took a little longer to find him. But Adrian was certainly worth the wait."

They met at church through their minister and both instantly knew this was something special. She describes a feeling of magic they both shared, which continued throughout their relatively short time together. "When we met, sparks flew! He was indeed a true blessing in my life. Our partnership was one of total unity. We shared so much in common and each and every day we spent together was a wonderful gift I will always cherish."

Margaret was a beautiful bride and celebrated with all the typical traditions. She excitedly made plans for their wedding day, had bridal showers and even shopped for the perfect wedding gown.

 "The gown was exquisite . . . long and white with a lovely train, and a delicate little veil," Margaret said. "The flowers, the guest list, the music, the ceremony were all so wonderful . . . just like every bride dreams of. We had brides-maids, groomsmen, and children from the bell choir per-formed the music, which was just absolutely angelic. One thing about getting married later in life, however, is that there are a lot of guests. We had more than three hundred in the church, so it was indeed a day of special memories and a glo-rious occasion."

Their newlywed life was similar to any other, according to Margaret. She knows this may be surprising, but she believes it's important for people to know that intimacy is life long and is something that people can experience and enjoy all of their lives, regardless of their chronological age. "He too had a background in medicine, so we shared scientific interests as well as social and environmental issues. We both enjoyed reading and every morning read the Bible together. We loved hiking and did a fair amount before his health declined. We traveled, adventured, and experienced life together. He came to my sixtieth college reunion, and I accompanied him to England for one of his. It was indeed a beautiful union that I will always be very thankful for."

They were only able to share four short years together before Adrian died, but he will never be forgotten, because Margaret created the Jones-Kanaar Foundation in his memory. Dedicated to youth and assisting people with CP, the foundation supports programs for the physically challenged and grants awards for volunteerism at local high schools. Additionally, Margaret's most recent venture is the development of the Reading Picture Book for Toddlers, because she believes that children can learn an amazing amount in the first three years of life with appropriate learning tools and good parent-child bonding.

"There is still much to do to improve the lives of others. Whether it's through my activities in the church and my community or the research projects for CP, the importance of continuing to contribute and make things happen is what inspires me to keep doing every day. Mental stimulation is so essential throughout our lives, and once you give that up and lose interest in the world around you, it's all downhill from there."

Dr. Margaret Jones-Kanaar is one who makes things happen, and she has no intention of stopping her contributions anytime soon. Engagement keeps you connected to life . . . and life is definitely her true passion.

Jack LaLanne, 83

꙳

The 'Godfather of Fitness'

W e all want to stay healthy, prevent disease, and maintain an activity level of vigor and vitality in our lives. But are we willing to do the work, or rather the workout, in order to achieve it? If it's motivation you need, there are few more inspiring than Jack LaLanne. Known to many as the "Godfather of Fitness," Jack continues his commitment to health and wellness in a way that is inspirational to one and all, regardless of age.

Age has obviously not slowed Jack down. He's in great shape, rising daily at 5 A.M. to perform a two-hour workout, followed by a breakfast of carrot-celery juice, banana, apple, and protein powder. He still performs the extraordinarily difficult military-style fingertip push-ups, and his biceps and stomach muscles are hard as rocks -- even after all these years. He celebrated his 60th birthday with a two-mile swim across San Francisco Bay, handcuffed and ankles shackled, tugging a sand-filled one thousand-pound dinghy. For his 70th, he swam a mile through Long Beach Harbor; again in handcuffs and leg irons, but this time he tugged seventy rowboats, each with an occupant!

"Just because I'm who I am, people think it's easy and that I live to exercise," Jack said. "I do like how I feel and enjoy my good health, but it takes discipline. I have that same little devil sitting on my shoulder too, constantly giving me excuses to not work out. But I know better. It's an essential part of my life; it energizes me every day. So why not continue doing something that is so beneficial?"

Although he is recognized as the original health and fitness guru, proprietor of the first health club, inventor of weight machines, and originator of the exercise video, Jack didn't start his life out in a very healthy way. In fact, in his youth he called himself a "junk-food junkie". He says that he was actually a sugarholic, but fortunately turned it around after hearing a nutrition lecture that changed his life.

"I was 15 at the time and my poor eating habits were making me weak, mean, and sick. I suffered with all sorts of physical ills, including headaches and bulimia. Sugar in the body is like alcohol. It destroys all the B vitamins, which makes you irritable and unable to think right. I realized that I had a choice in how I felt, so right then and there I made a commitment to change my lifestyle and build a totally new Jack LaLanne!"

Jack studied everything he could get his hands on about nutrition and fitness. He was pre-med in college but graduated as a doctor of chiropractic due to his insatiable interest in helping people with prevention, before they became ill. "I decided to focus on chiropractic because there was more emphasis on the natural methods. My original goal was to become a doctor, but they were more into drugs, drugs, drugs, and I thought there was a better way."

So Jack went right to work on proving there was a better way, and it was exercise. He opened the nation's first heath club in Oakland, California, in 1936 at age 21, and named it the Jack LaLanne Physical Culture Studio. Not only was it America's first health spa, but the very first modern health spa in the world. There was nothing else like it, anywhere.

"This was the first progressive exercise studio that actually had people working out with weights, barbells and machines. I was the first to advocate weight resistance training, which is very common now, but wasn't then. In fact, most people thought I was simply nuts. But I forged ahead anyway and developed the first models of exercise equipment that have become standard in today's health spas, including leg-extension machines, pulley machines using cables, and the first weight selectors."

Jack was a pioneer with his crusade to promote the benefits of resistance-training exercises to improve health. He remembers when doctors told people that working out with weights would lead to heart attacks, a lowered sex drive, and that women would start to look like men. Today, with the abundance of research touting the benefits of strength training, combined with the growing numbers of world-class athletes who now work out with weights, Jack should be considered as much a visionary as he is a pioneer.

He continued to spread his message about the benefits of exercise through the powerful medium of television: "The Jack LaLanne Show" first aired in 1951. Young Jack knew that few people would be enthusiastic about exercising, so he had a gimmick. Happy, a beautiful white German shepherd appeared with him on the air. Recognizing that children were his initial audience, and that they controlled the television in the morning, he instinctively knew they would love the dog, and therefore would watch the show. "That's how we made the show personal, by embracing the kids and encouraging them to go get their mom, dad, grandmother, grandfather, or anybody else who was in the house to come out and exercise with Uncle Jack and Happy on TV. Not wanting to disappoint the kids, the adults exercised too. It was all part of the plan and is really how it all began."

The Jack LaLanne Show aired for eight years and went into national syndication in 1959, where it stayed until 1985. In total, Jack exercised on TV five days a week for thirty-four years! During that time, he also opened his own gyms and franchised a number of spas under the Jack LaLanne name. He has written several books, produced a variety of exercise videos, and still maintains his own business, Be Fit Enterprises, all in support of his efforts to promote health and fitness for people of all ages.

His wife Elaine is also a health and fitness advocate in her own right. She has shared the benefits of exercise with the masses as an instructor, on videos, and in her books. Happily married for thirty-nine years, Jack and Elaine are a team who encourage people to take care of the most important person in the world: themselves.

"The advice is plain and simple, and there are two primary rules," Jack said. "First, if man makes it, don't eat it . . . and if it tastes good, spit it out!" Elaine added, "Jack's as serious about diet as he is exercise. He is the most disciplined person I've ever met when it comes to eating habits. He will not eat between meals, and he won't eat hors d'oeuvres or even take a bite of birthday cake. We do enjoy a couple of glasses of wine with our dinner, because in moderation it's supposed to be good for our health."

Jack knows the benefits of a good diet, so he fuels his body with legumes, brown rice, whole-grain bread, lentils, hard-boiled egg whites, olive oil, and fruits. He is also adamant about his vitamins and supplements -- he takes "hundreds" of them, including all the antioxidants, vitamin C, alfalfa, watercress, parsley, garlic, and many other herbs as well.

"The second rule is: you've got to make exercise a part of your day -- the older you are, the more you should do," Jack said. As a founding member of the Governor's Council on Physical Fitness and Sports, Jack's primary interest is in addressing the large percentage of the population who disdain regular exercise. "We've got to teach people that exercise improves your quality of life by enabling you to live longer and healthier. Education is key, particularly in the area of fitness and aging. Exercise has been proven to delay age-related declines while helping to lessen the pain and debilitation of many conditions people automatically blame on age. It's not necessarily all the fault of age."

Unquestionably still considered by many to be America's health superstar, Jack personifies the secret of healthy aging, and he knows how to keep the body strong and on the go longer. He continues to lead by example and has also maintained his fun sense of humor throughout the process.

"We're all interested in saving time, and I think we've found a way to do that -- by living longer. Plus, I can't die; it would ruin my image!"

Ben Levinson, 103

&

Strength Training at 100

Life's a journey, and it's not the destination that matters as much as the trip along the way. Ben's been on an incredible journey, and he has no plans to fade into the sunset anytime soon. He's of the rare breed who has lived in three different centuries: the 1800s (Ben was born in 1895); the 1900s; and the new millennium!

"I'm 103-years young, not old!" Ben said. "I'm a recycled teenager. People always want to know how I've lived so long, and I simply tell them -- breathe!" he laughed. "But in all seriousness, staying active has been the secret to my long life . . . with a little luck and good fortune added in too."

Call it luck, call it fate, call it hard work -- all play a role in Ben's current challenge: to continue enjoying his independence and quality of life by slowing down the aging process and in some ways actually reversing it. Exercise has

been a key component in this effort, and has unquestionably made a significant difference in improving Ben's life. "I'm not just existing anymore, I'm living," Ben stated. "I feel better and am stronger now, at 103, then I was at 100. And it's all because of this exercise I'm doing and the new things I've learned about strength training and its effect on balance and mobility, which enables me to keep doing the things I like and stay independent."

It all started when a mutual friend introduced Ben to Bob Delaney, 55. With a background in health and fitness, Bob was not only amazed at Ben's abilities at the age of 100, but he was also concerned that trouble could be lurking around the bend for Ben. "He was beginning to have some difficulty walking, which was interfering with the quality of his active lifestyle," Bob said. "He was starting to really go downhill primarily due to declining muscle mass in his legs. His balance was off, and he was having a hard time getting up out of a chair. I was confident we could slow down the muscle loss with proper exercise, so I encouraged Ben to give it a try."

Bob told Ben about the latest research and referred him to the book Biomarkers: The 10 Keys To Prolonging Vitality, by William Evans, Ph.D., and Irwin H. Rosenberg, M.D. Their studies showed that exercise provided significant improvements in 70-, 80-, and 90-year olds' abilities.

Although Ben had been active all his life, it was hard even for him to believe exercise could make such a difference. Since he had played tennis for more than fifty years, Bob helped him recognize that advances in strength-training research were similar to those fancy titanium tennis rackets that have replaced the wooden ones Ben used to play with. "That was a good analogy, and it made perfect sense to me," Ben said. "But I didn't want to be some guinea pig some-where that was just experimenting with new stuff. I was inter-ested in a professional, quality, training site, with researchers."

Bob found the Ruby Gerontology Center at California State University at Fullerton (CSUF), which had a state-of-the-art program. Before getting started, Ben and Bob wanted the support of Ben's doctor, who was actually more difficult to convince than Ben. "At first, the doctor's attitude was, 'Hey . . . the guy's 100, he's obviously done something right -- just let him be,'" Bob said. "The doctor also felt this was simply just natural progression for someone his age. Nothing could stop it, and it was a waste of time to try."

But Ben felt differently. The research material convinced him that Bob was right. He was headed for a fall unless he improved his balance and mobility. And so the journey began. Twice a week Ben and Bob made the 100-mile round-trip trek to the Lifespan Wellness Clinic at CSUF, where they were introduced to co-directors Drs. Jessie Jones and Roberta Rikli. The primary mission of the Lifespan program and research is to prevent frailty in older adults through a unique program focusing on exercise, strength training, and mobility exercises.

"I was impressed with the philosophy and the program. And although I'd never worked out with weights before, I began to understand just how important strength is to one's balance and ability to get around. Being physically active is a major contributor to maintaining one's independence and quality of life," Ben said.

Improving quality of life and enabling people to maintain their independence as long as possible in order to continue participating in all the activities in their lives, is the goal of the Lifespan Wellness program. And it definitely succeeded in making this a reality for Ben.

"One of the most important things Ben learned in this program was that he has some influence over his quality of life," Bob said. "He learned leg strength is key to his balance and independence. When the legs go because of declining

muscle strength, it can start a domino effect. You don't get up
and around as much, then the balance goes, which sets you up
for a fall, and then it's just one problem after the next. When I
lost fifty pounds, the majority of my back problems disap-
peared right along with the extra weight, and now I feel great.
So we give credence to the fact that lifestyle changes definitely work!"

Ben claims he has more energy now than he's ever
had. Even his doctor is quite impressed with his improve-
ment. And although Ben still has to deal with his share of
health challenges, he knows he's doing better now than he was
before. Additionally, he believes more people need to be
aware of the quality-of-life benefits exercise can provide, for
people of all ages.

"The results have really been remarkable. You should
see me pop out of the chair now -- like a bagel out of a toast-
er!" Ben proudly said.

"I'm living proof exercise works, at any age!" Ben
said. "And I think this is important, not just for the personal
benefits, but also in understanding the economic value of personal responsibility for health, wellness and prevention. Our
country is facing an expensive health care challenge, but we
can help by taking better care of ourselves so we don't overuse
the system. There's a lot we can do to combat the frailties and
costs of aging, and people need to realize this and take action.
Maybe we can save some Medicare dollars and increase a person's quality of life - that's a winning combination!"

So while Ben continues his incredible journey, (and
he's optimistic he'll be on this trail a while), may he also experience and enjoy all life has to offer along the way.

Bert Morrow, 85

&

World Record Hurdler

S ome things never change with age. Maintaining a
healthy diet and exercising regularly have proven to be
important for all ages. Keeping mentally fit also plays
a role, as does keeping oneself challenged. Yet the challenges
85-year old Bert Morrow discusses make you forget all about
age. Maybe that's the real secret of aging well -- not thinking
about your age, but just do it!

To say things get better with age is an understatement
for this athletic gent who didn't even start competing until the
young age of 69. Since that time, Bert has become something
of a senior track-star legend. He has been the recipient of
more than 29 world championship medals and 115 medals
from the U.S. National Championships. He first broke the
Masters world record in the 80-meter hurdles at age 76, and
the U.S. record for the 300-meter hurdles at age 81 and
recently, Bert set three new American and world records in the
80m Sprint, 80m Hurdles, and the 200m Sprint at the National
Indoor Track & Field Championships. His athletic accomplishments also landed him the star role in an award-winning
national television commercial for Chiquita bananas.

Bert is about as modest as one gets. "It's not about the
medals and records, it's about the challenge, the competition,
and always trying to do your best," he said. This ageless philosophy apparently works, because Bert claims he is in the

best shape of his life. And there's little doubt in his mind that diet and exercise have been key to his success in both competition and overall good health.

His diet is one Euell Gibbons would be proud of, since it consists mainly of fruits, grains, and vegetables. His breakfast begins the night before when he soaks a mixture of thirteen raw grains overnight. In the morning he drains off the liquid and tops the combo off with honey, banana, and bee pollen. His liquid refreshment is equally intriguing, the "aloe vera cocktail," with a squeeze of lime or a twist of lemon added to this juice-and-hot water concoction that Bert's been drinking for more than twenty-five years. He was apparently ahead of his time with this concept, because aloe vera juice is now being touted for its exceptional antioxidant powers.

Exercises start off the day, with his first stretches being done in his bed. Then it's on to the "Gravity Gizmo," (a HangUp inversion table) which Bert straps himself into and hangs upside down from while performing sixty sit-ups, bringing his hands up to touch his toes that helps strengthen his stomach, back, hips, and waist, what Bert refers to as "the core" of the body. Following this ritual, the day continues with more stretching on the floor, totaling thirty minutes in all. It's a routine he swears by and says nothing ever gets in the way of!

"I don't think people have any idea how important flexibility and stretching are to being able to move, prevent falls, and just plain get around," said Bert. "And it's particularly important as one gets older, since it's generally pain and stiffness people complain about and blame on old age. In many cases, it's simply not enough movement that's the real problem."

Bert believes movement is key to rejuvenating the cells in the body and staying healthy. He remembers reading

about it in a book once, and he personally experienced the phenomenon several years ago when he first retired and had a 53-foot Ketch built so that he and his wife could set out and see the world.

"We sailed 19,000 miles in three years. We were in the best shape of our lives when we returned because of the constant moving on the boat. Even when you're sleeping in your bunk, the ocean motion is continually moving your body, rejuvenating those cells, and making you feel great. I'm convinced there is definitely something beneficial about movement!"

Getting enough movement has become a daily priority for Bert. His weekly regimen includes two days of track work for speed and hurdles, and three days a week at a local university gym for his hour strength-training workout, which he also credits to improving his speed on the track. In fact, Bert improved his hurdle time from last year in a recent track and field event competition, so those who think that one can't improve with age better check again!

"We do need to think differently about what's possible with age because mental elements play a key role," Bert said. "I credit my never give up mindset to something my grandfather said: "The difficult is easy; the impossible just takes a little longer.'"

Bert believes nothing is impossible if you try and he gives new meaning to the saying, "some things never change with age!"

Virginia Shaver, 76

&

Septuagenarian Student

She'd always wanted to go back to school and earn her college degree, preferably in communications. Virginia had long dreamed of becoming a writer, but she also dreamed of living a long happy life with her husband of fifty years. When he died of cancer and her life was turned upside down, she decided to make a positive change -- so off to school she went. Enrolling at Missouri Southern State College, Virginia made history by becoming the oldest student on record, and the oldest dorm resident, too! It was an experience and the education of a lifetime, for everyone involved.

"I didn't know if my brain was going to be up to the challenge, especially having not been in school for more than fifty-two years," Virginia said. "But I'm happy to report that the old brain is the best computer in the world. Nothing compares; it worked like a champ! I wonder how many computers around today will still be current and functioning as well in fifty-two years!"

To save making a daily 75-mile round-trip commute, Virginia decided to move into a dorm on campus and go home on the weekends. She swapped her sprawling farmhouse for a dorm room and brought all the comforts of home with her: an Oriental rug, photos of her eight grand-children and nine great-grandchildren, and an electric skillet for cooking fried potatoes, her favorite food.

"I became the resident grandma, literally, and I encouraged the girls to visit anytime they wanted. I never felt like a misfit, I was one of the girls -- just a little bit older! We had a great time-shared popcorn, stories, and since I was also the only one with a car, having wheels made me a really big hit! We went all sorts of places!"

Virginia served as both a mentor and a friend. She talked with one very homesick student until three in the morning, played matchmaker for another, and even helped one friend write a paper on the Great Depression. Faculty, friends and family were always there to support Virginia, too. When her health problems made school a challenge and almost forced her to quit, they all rallied behind her and encouraged her to finish.

Although Virginia's health made her feel like giving up, it also reminded her of how she felt when her husband died and why she embarked on this endeavor in the first place. "When you go through the loss of a spouse, it's like part of your life has died too. You're so overwhelmed with emotion and feel like there is nothing that will ever help you heal. Friends try to help, but when it comes right down to it, it's a totally personal process."

Virginia remembers how a book entitled, To Live Again, by Genevieve Davis Ginsberg, who founded the Widow to Widow program helped her. "The secret is to build a new life, to always keep yourself open to new things and stay positive. At first this seems impossible, I know, because you don't want to build a new life, you want your old one back. But eventually you realize that's just not possible, and this is what you have to do to go on."

Virginia did complete her degree and graduated with the others to a standing ovation. Her health is also coming back, and she's confident she'll achieve her goal of writing inspirational articles for religious magazines.

"You've got to feel good in order to want to do anything, but you've also got to do things in order to feel good!" Virginia said. "I've learned that I can do this. Even when challenges do arise, I can overcome them if I just always continue to try."

And that may very well just be the lesson for a lifetime.

Lowell Tozer, 76

୫୦

Cuddler Volunteer

S ome speak of "the Midas touch," but when people talk
about Lowell, they speak about "the special touch."
His enthusiasm for cuddling babies is a true act of
love, and it's one he says he would gladly pay to do if he
didn't have the opportunity as a volunteer. Lowell is special
and he's found the perfect job: to cuddle and love premature
babies as one of only three men enrolled in a University
Medical Center's Cuddler's Program.

"I've always loved babies, ask my family," Lowell
said. "We'll all be out together, at a restaurant or wherever,
talking away, and all of a sudden I'll spot a baby across the
room and they lose me, I become totally enthralled. My family just smiles and says, 'Oh, no . . . there goes Dad again . . .
he's found another baby!'"

There's no question the human touch is essential and
even therapeutic for babies, but cuddling infants is not something you find many men doing. It seems more often women
this type of nurturing is done by women. "It isn't your typical
macho occupation, but I believe there are many men like me
out there who would love to be involved in something like
this," Lowell said. "In fact, a newspaper article recently
appeared about the male Cuddlers which swamped the hospital staff with phone calls from numerous other men who also
wanted to get involved."

Call it luck, good timing, or maybe even divine intervention, because when Lowell called about the Cuddler program, not only was there a rare opening for a new volunteer, but the training course for the rookies was scheduled to begin the very next day. Lowell was definitely at the right place at the right time.

"This was my first volunteer job ever. And I'll tell you, if I had known I could be doing this in retirement, I would have retired a lot sooner! I started four years ago and they're going to have to kick me out, because I have no intention of ever leaving. In fact, the standard volunteer shift is three hours per week, but that just wasn't enough for me. I talked them into letting me come three days a week and I absolutely love it!"

Although Lowell recognizes that babies are his weakness, it is oftentimes the baby's weakness that really gets Lowell's attention. Whether it's those who are premature or those with serious medical problems, they all need loving and cuddling, and Lowell is always at the ready.

"We bundle them up in their blanket like a little burrito and hold them close to our bodies, which in my case radiates a lot of warmth because of my metabolism," Lowell explained. "And with the preemies (premature babies), sometimes I'll put a blanket over their head to block out the lights and whisper to them: 'we'll just pretend you're not born yet.'"

Lowell also enjoys running and playing the piano. Although he's been on a two-year sabbatical from competitive running due to an annoying arthritic hip joint that the doctors say will only be repaired with replacement surgery, he is making a comeback with orthotics in his shoes and a couple of natural supplements that seem to be helping to improve his condition.

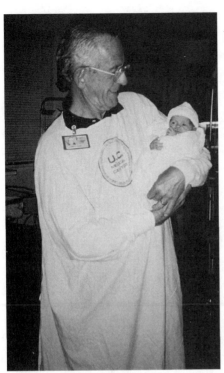

Lowell keeps his brain busy, too, by playing the piano again after a forty-year lapse. He admits he was fairly talented in his youth, and was amazed that his skills came back relatively easily, which proved to Lowell that the mind and memory might not always decline over time. "I have a great memory . . . always did and still do! But I think staying engaged keeps you alive. Over the last three years I've been reading books on the mind and its abilities, which has led me to books on consciousness, evolution, quantum physics, and complexity theory. There's definitely a connection between keeping your mind and body active throughout your lifetime, and continuing to learn, regardless of age. I can't imagine life without curiosity, keeping my brain and mind actively engaged."

Lowell admits that he has no idea what the secret to long life is, other than just taking care of yourself and staying involved. Giving is also rewarding. "One of the most beneficial things in the world is giving love, so volunteering to love those babies is very fulfilling," Lowell said. "Sometimes I actually feel guilty because I think I'm getting more out of this than the babies. There seems to be a magical connection between us -- I'm sure they sense that I love them, because I really truly do!"

RESOURCES

AARP - AMERICAN ASSOCIATION OF RETIRED
PERSONS
601 E Street NW, Washington, DC 20049 · (800) 424-3410 ·
202-434-2277

AARP - NORTHEAST REGION
One Boston Place, Ste 1900, Boston MA 02108 · 617-723-
7600

AARP - SOUTHEAST REGION
999 Peachtree Street NE, Ste 2650, Atlanta GA 30309 · 404-
888-0077

AARP - MIDWEST REGION
8750 West Bryn Mawr Avenue, Ste 600, Chicago IL 60631
773-714-9800

AARP - SOUTHWEST REGION
8144 Walnut Hill Lane, Ste 700 LB-39, Dallas TX 75231-
4316 · 214-265-4060

AARP - WEST REGION
9750 Third Avenue NE, Ste 400, Seattle WA 98115
206-526-7918

AARP VOLUNTEER TALENT BANK
800-727-7788 · Referral for local affiliate and opportunities

ADVENTURE CYCLING ASSOCIATION
P.O. Box 8308-P, Missoula MT 59807 · 406-721-1776

AEROBICS AND FITNESS ASSOCIATION OF AMERICA
15250 Ventura Blvd., Ste 200, Sherman Oaks CA 91403
818-905-0040

AMATEUR ATHLETIC UNION (AAU)
Walt Disney Resorts, P.O. Box 10000, Lake Buena Vista FL
32830 · 407-363-6170

AMATEUR SPEEDSKATING UNION OF THE UNITED
STATES
1033 Shady Lane, Glen Ellyn IL 60137-4822 · 630-790-3230

AMERICAN ACADEMY OF MEDICAL ACUPUNCTURE
800-521-2262 · Referral for local contact

AMERICAN ALLIANCE FOR HEALTH, PHYSICAL
EDUC., RECREATION & DANCE
1900 Association Dr, Reston VA 20191 · 703-476-3400 ·
http://www.aahperd.org/

AMERICAN ALPINE CLUB
710 10th Street, Golden CO 80401 · 303-384-0110

AMERICAN ASSOC. OF CARDIOVASCULAR & PUL-
MONARY REHABILITATION
7611 Elmwood Avenue, Ste 201, Middleton WI 53562
608-831-6989

AMERICAN BOWLING CONGRESS
5301 South 76 Street, Greendale WI 53129 · 414-421-6400

AMERICAN CANCER SOCIETY
1599 Clifton Road NE, Atlanta GA 30329-4251 · 800-227-
2345 · 404-320-3333

AMERICAN COLLEGE OF SPORTS MEDICINE
P.O. Box 1440, Indianapolis IN 46206-1440 · 800-486-5643 ·
317-637-9200

AMERICAN COLLEGE OF SURGEONS
55 E. Erie Street, Chicago IL 60611 · 312-664-4070

AMERICAN COUNCIL ON EXERCISE (ACE)
5820 Oberlin Dr Ste 102, San Diego CA 92121 · 800-825-
3636 · 619-535-8227

AMERICAN DIABETES ASSOCIATION
1660 Duke Street, Alexandria VA 22314 · 800-DIA-BETES

AMERICAN DIETETIC ASSOCIATION
216 W. Jackson Blvd., Ste 800, Chicago IL 60606-6995 · 800-
366-1655

AMERICAN FOUNDATION FOR THE BLIND
15 W. 16th Street, New York NY 10011 · 800-232-5463

AMERICAN GERIATRICS SOCIETY
770 Lexington Avenue, Ste 300, New York NY 10021 · 212-
308-1414

AMERICAN HEART ASSOCIATION
800-242-8721 o For referral to local affiliate o
http://www.amhrt.org/
7272 Greenville Avenue, Dallas TX 75231 · 214-706-1936

AMERICAN LUNG ASSOCIATION
1740 Broadway, New York NY 10010 · 212-315-8700

AMERICAN MEDICAL ASSOCIATION
515 North State Street, Chicago IL 60610 · 800-202-3211 ·
312-464-5000

AMERICAN OCCUPATIONAL THERAPY ASSOCIATION,
INC.
P.O. Box 31220, Bethesda MD 20824-3122 · 301-652-2682

AMERICAN ORTHOPAEDIC SOCIETY FOR SPORTS
MEDICINE (AOSSM)
6300 N. River Road, Ste 200, Rosemont IL 60018 · 847-292-
4900

AMERICAN PARKINSON'S DISEASE ASSOCIATION
60 Bay Street, Ste 401, Straten Island NY 10301 · 800-223-2732

AMERICAN PHYSICAL THERAPY ASSOCIATION
1111 N. Fiarfax Street, Alexandria VA 22314 · 703-684-2782

AMERICAN PLATFORM TENNIS ASSOCIATION
P.O. Box 43336, Upper Montclair NJ 07043 · 201-744-1190

AMERICAN RACEWALK ASSOCIATION
P.O. Box 4, Paonia CO 81428 · 970-527-4557

AMERICAN RED CROSS
18 D Street NW, Washington DC 20006 · 202-737-8300

AMERICAN RUNNING & FITNESS ASSOCIATION
4405 East-West Hwy, Ste 405, Bethesda MD 20814-1621 · 301-913-9517

AMERICAN SELF PROTECTION ASSOCIATION, INC.
(Judo, Aikido, Tai Chi)
825 Greengate Oval, Sagamore Hills OH 44067 · 330-467-1750

AMERICAN SOCIETY ON AGING
833 Market Street, Ste 500, San Francisco CA 94103 · 415-974-9600

AMERICAN SOCIETY OF BIOMECHANICS
Orthopaedic Biomechanics Lab, 128 Guggenheim, Mayo Clinic
Rochester MN 55905 · 507-284-2262

AMERICAN SWIM COACHES ASSOCIATION
301 S.E. 20th Street, Ft. Lauderdale FL 33316 · 954-462-6267

AMERICAN WATER SKI ASSOCIATION
799 Overlook Drive, Winterhaven FL 33884 · 800-533-2972

ARTHRITIS FOUNDATION
1314 Spring Street, Atlanta GA 30309 · 800-283-7800

BE FIT ENTERPRISES - Jack LaLanne Products
P.O. Box 1023 o San Luis Obispo CA 93406 · 805-772-6000

CALIFORNIA PARKS & RECREATION SOCIETY
916-665-2777 · http://www.cprs.org

CALIFORNIA STATE UNIVERSITY FULLERTON (CSUF)
Lifespan Wellness Center, Fullerton CA 92634 · 714-278-2620

CANADIAN ASSOC. FOR HEALTH, PHYSICAL EDUC.,
RECREATION & DANCE
1600 James Naismith Dr, Gloucester, Ontario, Canada K1B
5N4 · 613-748-5622

CANADIAN FITNESS & LIFESTYLE RESEARCH
INSTITUTE
201-185 Somerset St. West, Ottawa, Ontario, Canada K2P 0J2
613-233-5528

CANADIAN SOCIETY FOR EXERCISE PHYSIOLOGY
185 Somerset St. West #202, Ottawa, Ontario, Canada K2P
0J2 · 613-234-3755

CENTER FOR DISEASE CONTROL AND PREVENTION
1600 Clifton Road NE, Atlanta GA 30383
888-232-4674 · 404-639-3311

CENTER FOR THE STUDY OF AGING
706 Madison Avenue, Albany NY 12208 · 518-465-6927

COOPER INSTITUTE FOR AEROBIC RESEARCH
12330 Preston Road, Dallas TX 75230 · 972-701-8001

DISABLED SPORTS USA
451 Hungerford Drive, Ste 100, Rockville MD 20850
301-217-0960

ELDERHOSTEL
75 Federal Street, Boston MA 02110-194
617-426-8056 · 617-426-7788

FIFTY-PLUS FITNESS ASSOCIATION
Box D, Stanford CA 94309
650-323-6160 · www.50plus.org

FOSTER GRANDPARENTS
(800)645-3016 For referral to a local affiliate

GERONTOLOGIC SOCIETY OF AMERICA
1275 K Street NW, Ste 350, Washington DC 20005
202-842-1275

GRANDPARENTS UNITED FOR CHILDREN'S RIGHTS
INC. 137 Larkin Street, Madison WI 53705
sedun@inexpress.net

GRANDTRAVEL (Special Vacations for Grandparents &
Grandchildren)
6900 Wisconsin Avenue, Ste 706, Chevy Chase MD 20815 ·
800-247-7651

GRAY PANTHERS
2025 Pennsylvania Ave NW, Ste 821, Washington DC 20006 ·
800-280-5362

ICE SKATING INSTITUTE
355 West Dundee Road, Buffalo Grove IL 60089 · 847-808-
7528

IDEA - INTERNATIONAL ASSOCIATION OF FITNESS
PROFESSIONALS
6190 Cornerstone Ct East, Ste 204, San Diego CA 92121-
3773 · 619-535-8979

IHRSA - INT'L. HEALTH, RACQUET AND SPORTSCLUB
ASSOCIATION
263 Summer Street, Boston MA 02210 · 800-228-4772

INTERNATIONAL JUGGLERS ASSOCIATION
P.O. Box 218, Montague MA 01351 · 413-367-2401

INTERNATIONAL PHYSICAL FITNESS ASSOCIATION
415 W. Court Street, Flint MI 48503 · 810-239-2166

INTERNATIONAL SENIOR SOFTBALL ASSOCIATION
9303 Center Street, Manasa VA 20110 · 703-368-1188

INTERNATIONAL SWIMMING HALL OF FAME
One Hall of Fame Drive, Ft. Lauderdale FL 33316 · 954-462-
6536

INTERNATIONAL WEIGHTLIFTING ASSOCIATION
P.O. Box 444, Hudson OH 44236 · 216-655-9644

JAZZERCISE, INC.
2808 Roosevelt Street, Carlsbad CA 92008 · 760-434-2101

LEAGUE OF AMERICAN BICYCLISTS
190 W. Ostend Street, Ste 120, Baltimore MD 21230 · 410-
539-3399

MEN'S SENIOR BASEBALL LEAGUE
1 Huntington Quadrangle, Ste 3N07, Melville NY 11747 ·
516-753-6725

NATIONAL ALLIANCE FOR SENIOR CITIZENS
1700 18th Street NW, Washington DC 20009 · 202-986-0117

NATIONAL ASSOCIATION OF AGEA AGENCIES ON
AGING
1112 16th Street NW, Ste 100, Washington DC 20036-4823 ·
202-296-8130

NATIONAL ASSOCIATION OF GOVERNOR'S COUNCIL
ON PHYSICAL FITNESS & SPORTS
201 S. Capitol Avenue, Ste 560, Indinanapolis IN 46255

NATIONAL ASSOCIATION OF SENIOR FRIENDS
P.O. Box 1300, Nashville TN 37202 · 800-348-4886

NATIONAL ASSOCIATION OF STATE UNITS ON AGING
12251 I Street NW, Ste 725, Washington DC 20005-3914 ·
202-898-2578

NATIONAL CONGRESS OF STATE GAMES & MEMBER
STATES
401 Ninth 31 Street, Billings MT 59101 · 406-254-7426

NATIONAL COUNCIL ON AGING
409 Third Street SW, Washington DC 20024-3212 · 202-479-
1200

NATIONAL COUNCIL ON SENIOR CITIZENS
1331 F Street NW, Washington DC 20004 · 202-347-8800

NATIONAL EYE INSTITUTE - INFORMATION OFFICE
Bldg 31 Room 6A32, 31 Center Drive, MSC 2510, Bethesda
MD 20892-2510 · 301-496-5248

NATIONAL HANDICAPPED SPORTS
916-989-0402 · Physical fitness activities for people with disabilities

NATIONAL HORSESHOE PITCHERS ASSOCIATION
3085 76 Street, Franksville WI 53126 · 414-835-9108

NATIONAL INSTITUTE ON AGING
Box 8057, Gaithersburg MD 20858 · 800-222-2225 · 301-496-1752

NATIONAL MASTERS NEWS (Track & Field, Long-Distance, Racewalking)
P.O. Box 50098, Eugene OR 97405 · 541-343-7716

NATIONAL OSTEOPOROSIS FOUNDATION
1150 17th Street NW, Ste 500, Washington DC 20036-4603 · 202-223-2226

NATIONAL RECREATION AND PARK ASSOCIATION
2775 So. Quincy Street, Ste 300, Arlington VA 22206 · 703-820-4940

NATIONAL SENIOR GAMES HEADQUARTERS
800-331-9211 · For referral to local affiliate

NATIONAL SENIOR PRO RODEO ASSOCIATION
P.O. Box 316, Roundup MT 59072 · 406-323-3380

NATIONAL SENIOR SERVICE CORPS HOTLINE
800-424-8867 · For referral to local affiliate and volunteer opportunities

NATIONAL SENIOR SPORTS ASSOCIATION
83 Princeton Avenue, Hopewell NJ 08525 · 800-282-6772

NATIONAL SOCIETY TO PREVENT BLINDNESS
500 E. Remington Road, Schaumberg IL 60173 · 800-331-2020

NATIONAL STRENGTH & CONDITIONING
ASSOCIATION
P.O. Box 38909, Colorado Springs CO 80937 · 719-632-6722

NATIONAL STROKE ASSOCIATION
300 East Hampton Avenue, Englewood CO 80110 · 303-762-
9922

NORTH AMERICAN SENIOR CIRCUIT SOFTBALL
1204 West 46 Street, Richmond VA 23225 · 804-231-4254

NORTH AMERICAN TELEMARK ORGANIZATION
Box 44, Waitsfield VT 05673 · 800-835-3404

OASIS
7710 Carondelet, Ste 125, St. Louis MO 63105 · 314-862-
2933
Offering a variety of adult education opportunities nationwide

OLDER AMERICAN'S VOLUNTEER PROGRAMS
1100 Vermont Avenue NW, 6th Floor, Washington DC 20525 ·
202-606-1855

OLDER WOMEN'S LEAGUE (OWL)
666 11th Street NW, Ste 700, Washington DC 20001 · 800-
825-3695

PRESIDENT'S COUNCIL ON PHYSICAL FITNESS &
SPORTS
701 Pennsylvania Ave NW, Ste 250, Washington DC 20004-
2608 · 202-272-3421

PROFESSIONAL BOWLERS ASSOCIATION
1720 Merriman Road, Akron OH 44334 · 330-836-5568

PROJECT P.A.C.E.
San Diego State University · Department of Psychology
619-594-4815
(Physician Based Assessment & Consultant for Exercise)

RAILS TO TRAIL CONSERVANCY
1400 16th Street NW, Ste 300, Washington DC 20036
202-797-5400
(Converts abandoned rail corridors to trails)

ROAD RUNNERS CLUB OF AMERICA
1150 South Washington Street, Ste 250, Alexandria VA 22314
703-836-0558

RSVP - RETIRED & SENIOR VOLUNTEER PROGRAM
See AARP

SENIOR ATHLETES HALL OF FAME
723 Oakview Drive, Bradenton FL 34210 · 941-756-8808

SENIOR GAMES ASSOC. - NATIONAL HEADQUARTERS
445 North Boulevard, Ste 2001, Baton Rouge LA 70802 ·
504-379-7337
(Senior Olympics)

SENIOR NET
399 Arguello, San Francisco CA 94188 · 415-750-5030

SENIOR OLYMPICS - NATIONAL HEADQUARTERS
800-331-9211 · For referral to local affiliate

SENIOR SOFTBALL USA INC.
9 Fleet Court, Sacramento CA 95831 · 916-393-8566

SERVICE CORPS OF RETIRED EXECUTIVES, SMALL
BUSINESS ADMIN.
409 Third Street SW, Washington DC 20024 · 202-205-6762

SPECIAL OLYMPICS INTERNATIONAL
1325 "G" Street NW, Ste 500, Washington DC 20005 · 202-628-3630

SPORTING GOODS MANUFACTURER'S ASSOCIATION
200 Castlewood Drive, North Palm Beach FL 33408 · 561-842-4100

TRIATHLON FEDERATION USA
3595 E. Fountain Blvd., F-1, Colorado Springs CO 80910 · 719-597-2121

UNITED PARKINSON'S FOUNDATION
833 W. Washington Blvd., Chicago IL 60607

U.S.A. HOCKEY, INC.
4965 North 30 Street, Colorado Springs CO 80919 · 719-599-5500

U.S.A. KARATE FEDERATION INC.
1300 Kenmore Blvd., Akron OH 44314 · 330-753-3114

U.S.A. SOFTBALL
2801 N.E. 50th Street, Oklahoma City OK 73111 · 405-424-5266

U.S.A. TABLE TENNIS
One Olympic Plaza, Colorado Springs CO 80909 · 719-632-4583

U.S.A. VOLLEYBALL
3595 East Fountain Blvd., Ste I-2, Colorado Springs CO 80910 · 719-597-6307

UNITED SQUARE DANCERS OF AMERICA INC.
8913 Seaton Drive, Huntsville AL 35802 · 205-881-6044

U.S. ADMINISTRATION ON AGING
330 Independence Avenue SW, Washington DC 20547-0008 ·
202-619-0724

U.S. AKIDO FEDERATION
98 State Street, Northhampton MA 01060 · 413-586-7122

U.S. AMATEUR BALLROOM DANCERS ASSOCIATION
P.O. Box 428, New Freedom PA 17439 · 800-447-9047

U.S. AMATEUR ROLLER SKATERS
P.O. Box 6579, Lincoln NE 68506 · 402-483--7551
(Roller & In-Line Skating)

U.S. BADMITTON ASSOCIATION
One Olympic Plaza, Colorado Springs CO 80909 · 719-578-
4808

U.S. CEREBRAL PALSY ATHLETIC ASSOCIATION
200 Harrison Street, Newport RI 02840 · 401-848-2460

U.S. CROQUET ASSOCIATION
11585-B Polo Club Road, Wellington FL 33414 · 561-753-
9141

U.S. DEPARTMENT OF AGRICULTRUE - FOOD AND
CONSUMER INFORMATION
703-305-2286 · fnic@nalusda.gov

U.S. FENCING ASSOCIATION VETERANS PROGRAM
130 NE 26th Avenue, Ste 101, Boynton Beach FL 33435 ·
407-737-5595

U.S. FIELD HOCKEY ASSOCIATION
One Olympic Plaza, Colorado Springs CO 80909 · 719-578-
4567

U.S. FIGURE SKATING ASSOC. - ADULT PROGRAM
20 First Street, Colorado Springs CO 80906 · 719-635-9549

U.S. GOLF ASSOCIATION (USGA)
P.O. Box 708, Far Hills NJ 07931 · 908-234-2300

U.S. HANDBALL ASSOCIATION
2333 N. Tucson Blvd., Tucson AZ 85716 · 520-795-0465

U.S. JUDO ASSOCIATION
21 North Union Blvd., Colorado Springs CO 80919 · 719-633-7750

U.S. JUDO INC.
P.O. Box 10013, El Paso TX 79991 · 915-771-6699

U.S. MASTERS SWIMMING
2 Peter Avenue, Rutland MA 01543 · 508-886-6631

U.S. NATIONAL SENIOR SPORTS ORGANIZATION
1307 Washington Avenue, Ste 706, St. Louis MO 63103 · 314-621-5545

U.S. OLYMPIC SPORTS MEDICINE SOCIETY
1 Olympic Plaza, Colorado Springs CO 80909-5760 · 719-578-4546

U.S. PROFESSIONAL TENNIS ASSOCIATION (USPTA)
3535 Briarpark Drive, Houston TX 77402 · 713-978-7782

U.S. RECREATIONAL TENNIS ASSOCIATION
3112 Adderley Court, Silver Spring MD 20906 · 301-598-4820

U.S. ROWING ASSOCIATION
201 So. Capitol Avenue, Ste 400, Indianapolis IN 46225 · 317-237-5656

U.S. SLO-PITCH SOFTBALL ASSOCIATION
3935 S. Crater Road, Petersburg VA 23805 · 804-732-1704

U.S. SQUASH RACQUETS ASSOCIATION
23 Cynwyd Road, P.O. Box 1216, Bala Cynwyd PA 19004 ·
610-667-4006

U.S. SYNCHRONIZED SWIMMING
201 So. Capitol Avenue, Ste 510, Indianapolis IN 46225 ·
317-237-5700

U.S. TENNIS ASSOCIATION (USTA)
70 West Red Oak Lane, White Plains NY 10604 · 914-696-
7000

U.S. WALKING FEDERATION
4831 North East 44th Street, Seattle WA 98105 · 206-524-
6081

UNIVERSITY OF SOUTHERN CALIFORNIA (USC)
Ethel Percy Andrus Gerontology Center
Leonard Davis Volunteer Center
University Park - MC 0191, Los Angeles, CA 90089-0191 ·
213-740-6060

UNIVERSITY OF SOUTHERN CALIFORNIA (USC)
Master Athlete Study o Department of Exercise Sciences
University Park, Los Angeles, CA 90089-0652

WHEELCHAIR SPORTS, USA
3595 East Fountain Blvd., Ste L-1, Colorado Springs CO
80910 · 719-574-1150

WOMEN'S SPORTS FOUNDATION
Eisenhower Park, East Meadow NY 11554 · 516-542-4700

WORLD FOOTBALL ASSOCIATION
P.O. Box 775208, Steamboat Springs CO 80477 · 303-278-9797

WORLD MASTERS CROSS COUNTRY SKI ASSOC.
P.O. Box 5, Bend OR 97709 · 541-382-3505

YMCA OF THE USA
101 North Wacker Drive, Chicago IL 60606 · 800-872-9622 · 312-977-0031

YMCA OF THE USA
726 Broadway, New York NY 10003 · 212-614-2799

KELLY FERRIN
Gerontologist · Author · Speaker

Kelly is a gerontologist who has been studying aging and retirement issues for over 20 years. She was one of the first to ever receive a degree in this field, from the prestigious Andrus School of Gerontology at the University of Southern California, considered one of the top schools in the nation for the study of age-related issues.

Passionately committed to educating the public on longevity and healthy aging, Kelly started her own company, Lifestyles in 1986, where she serves as a consultant and motivational speaker to various organizations serving the senior market. From her work in the financial industry with longevity's effect on retirement planning to conducting Pre-Retirement programs for corporate clients, and providing keynote presentations at various conferences across the country, Kelly is sought out to motivate audiences with her powerfully engaging programs on new images of aging.

The United Nations and the World Health Organization recruited Kelly and her team of super seniors in a collaboration with the Sporting Goods Manufacturer's Association to celebrate the "International Year of the Older Person." The County of San Diego also contracted her to develop a unique wellness and fitness program, "The Feeling Fit Clubs" which has won numerous national awards including the 2003 American Society on Aging's Healthcare & Aging Award, and is now considered a statewide and national model. It also airs weekdays on cable TV. As a result of this work, Kelly was the recipient of the County's prestigious "Starfish Award" for excellence in community service in recognition of making a positive difference in people's lives.

In addition to being a certified AARP retirement specialist, local newspaper columnist, and elected consultant with the Governor's Council on Physical Fitness and Sports for older adults, Kelly has also co-produced a local cable television show, *Age Talk*, and her message has been shared internationally throughout Canada, England, and Australia.

One of her most attributed achievements that brought Kelly into the national spotlight was authoring her first internationally released book, *"What's Age Got To Do With It? Secrets to Aging In Extraordinary Ways."* Her upbeat message has also coined Kelly the "age angel" for her unique vision of the current and future older adult population which has been featured on both radio and TV talk shows nationwide. Her message on aging is both informative and inspiring, and by sharing the good news about aging, Kelly hopes to forever change the way people look at aging. . . and even how they age themselves.

To contact Kelly or for further information,
visit Kelly's website at:

www.ageangel.com

or

www.kellyferrin.com